THE TAL

# THE TA
## A STUDY OF JUDAISM

First Edition 1897
Arsene Darmesteter

New Edition 2019
Edited by Tarl Warwick

# THE TALMUD

## COPYRIGHT AND DISCLAIMER

The first edition of this work is in the public domain having been written prior to 1925. This edition, with its cover art and format, is all rights reserved.

In no way may this text be construed as encouraging or condoning any harmful or illegal act. In no way may this text be construed as able to diagnose, treat, cure, or prevent any disease, injury, symptom, or condition.

# THE TALMUD

## FOREWORD

This following booklet is a fairly broad but somewhat comprehensive treatment of Judaism's Talmud, its study and content, the sections thereof, and so forth. For those who have not studied Judaism (mystic or otherwise) the subject can be quite difficult- the Judaistic religion contains a strong legalistic and interpretative component often absent or more limited within other spiritual groups; we might consider the opinions of notable Rabbis on spiritual subjects as roughly akin to the opinions of some philosophers of Christendom, but the comparison is not, perhaps, complete. Indeed (and this work states the same) it is considered perhaps better to listen to the interpretations than to spend untold time delving through the Talmud itself to find meaning- dozens of pages being ascribed to each short statement.

For those who wish for the more straightly occult side of Judaism the Sepher Bahir and Sepher Yetzirah are quite important; it should be noted that this is a fairly modern text crafted specifically for the understanding of the basics of Judaism, along with numerous others, by the Jewish Publication Society, and does not represent depth so much as general scope for the understanding of the topic.

This edition of "The Talmud" has been carefully edited for format and word usage. Care has been taken to retain all original intent and meaning.

# THE TALMUD

## PREFATORY NOTE

The following passage from the biography of Arsene Darmesteter, prefixed to Volume I of his 'Reliques Scientifiques', deserves quotation, both on account of its criticism of Emanuel Deutsch's brilliant article on the Talmud, which originally appeared in the Quarterly Review for October, 1867 (reprinted as No. 3 of this Special Series), and as an illustration of the phenomenon, often noted in the scientific world, that investigators, wholly independent and perhaps in ignorance of each other, publish work of similar import simultaneously, though the phase of the subject presented may have been completely neglected up to that time.

The biographer, Arsene's equally distinguished brother, James Darmesteter, says (page xv): "In that period falls his first essay, an essay on the Talmud, in which he undertook to give an idea of the contents of that vast compilation, of its formation and its history, and which, even leaving out of consideration the age of the author,"- he was then about nineteen years old- "is a marvel by reason of its precision, clearness, and grasp of the subject. That essay might have sufficed to establish the reputation of an Orientalist and an historian. Unfortunately, Arsene did not find the means to publish it. As he was about to finish it, there appeared in an English review an article on the Talmud, treating in reality of scarcely anything but the Mishna, and written with perfect appreciation of the public to which the journal appealed. It is the model of a superficial, popular, enjoyable exposition. Deutsch's article created a sensation in England, and was translated in France. Coming after it, Arsene's, superior though it was, would have appeared to be inspired by it. It therefore remained unpublished despite the efforts later on

# THE TALMUD

made by M. Gaston Paris to effect its appearance in the French reviews... Notwithstanding the great and happy changes brought about in France during the last fifteen years in studies of this kind, which have found a center at the 'Ecole des Hautes Etudes' and an organ in the 'Revue des Etudes juives', his article has preserved its originality unimpaired, and even now is unique in our language as a summing up of the vast Talmudic chaos."

In a foot-note, the biographer says: "My brother later retouched his article, and introduced the references to Deutsch contained therein." The essay, here translated from the 'Reliques Scientifiques', finally, in 1889, the year following the death of its author, found its way into the 'Revue des Etudes juives.'

The Translator

# THE TALMUD

## THE TALMUD

The Talmud, exclusive of the vast Rabbinic literature attached to it, represents the uninterrupted work of Judaism from Ezra to the sixth century of the common era, the resultant of all the living forces and of the whole religious activity of a nation. If we consider that it is the faithful mirror of the manners, the institutions, the knowledge of the Jews, in a word of the whole of their civilization in Judea and Babylonia during the prolific centuries preceding and following the advent of Christianity, we shall understand the importance of a work, unique of its kind, in which a whole people has deposited its feelings, its beliefs, its soul. Nothing, indeed, can equal the importance of the Talmud, unless it be the ignorance that prevails concerning it. For what is generally known of this book. At the utmost its name. People have a vague idea that if is a huge, strange, fantastic work, written in a still more fantastic style, in which bits of all sorts of more or less exact knowledge, together with dreams and fables, lies heaped up with the incoherency of complete disorder. But it has not yet been made plain, that it is the work of a nation, the expression of a social system, and that in virtue thereof it falls under the laws governing the progress of humanity. It is not understood that it is a human product, whose origin and development are human, capable of being resolved into laws, and therefore laying claim to scientific analysis. From a very different point of view it has heretofore been studied. Up to the present, this word Talmud has had the power of kindling passions and exciting acrimonious strife.

The impartiality of which the author of the Annals boasts, *sine ira et studio*, should not be expected of those who have written about this book. I have not in mind the last three centuries, during which its study was oftenest inspired by religious passion; Christian scholars for the most part looking

# THE TALMUD

upon it as a monstrosity, an infernal production, which damned the morality of the Jewish people, and the Jews hotly defending the sacredness of a work that was the bulwark of their faith and the embodiment of their religious life. Even in our days, when the demand for a more scientific treatment is justified, the Talmud has in general not been accorded impartial criticism, which, rising above polemics, should examine it dispassionately, and consider its nature and growth in the spirit that the physiologist carries into the study of an animal or the philologist into that of the characters of a language. The Jews of Germany alone in the European world of scholars have built up the science of the Talmud by the application of the critical method, which was unknown to the Jewish historians of the middle ages. About forty years ago, Jost, Zunz, and Rapoport by their learned researches inaugurated the great movement that continues with unabated vigor in our own time. Many names suggest themselves; among others those of Krochmal, Herzfeld, Graetz, Frankel, and, above all, Geiger, who is remarkable for the assurance and the force of his bold criticism. Their influence is not confined to the Jewish world. Their work has succeeded in obtruding itself upon Protestant scholarship, both liberal and orthodox, forcing it to invite Talmudic research into the circle of the sciences. But outside of Germany their labors have met with only faint response. In France and England, they have been almost unknown up to the present time, and although special works are beginning to see the light of day, it is true that in the main nothing of these studies penetrates to the general public on this as on the other side of the Channel. For the benefit of this public, it is proposed in the following pages to give a cursory idea of the Talmud, by reviewing the principal results of German criticism. The first part shall be devoted to the analysis of the Talmud collection and to the examination of its two component elements, the Halacha (Ch pronounced as in the German Nacht.) and the Haggada.

# THE TALMUD

The second part is reserved for the history of the development of the book and of the laws governing it. Finally, after a glance at its vicissitudes during the middle ages and in modern times, we shall indicate what remains for science to do with the Talmud, and what science may expect to find in it for the history of mankind at large.

# THE TALMUD

## PART FIRST

## ANALYTIC SKETCH OF THE TALMUD

### I: GENERAL CHARACTERISTICS

If one of the heavy folios that constitute the Talmud collection be opened at random, the eye will be met by a text in the square Hebrew characters, which is framed on the right and left by narrow columns, and above and below by wide bands, of a finer text, printed in the Rabbinic characters. The frame is the work of French commentators of the middle ages; the portion framed is the TALMUD.

The Talmud, in turn, is composed of two distinct parts, the Mishna and the Gemara; the former the text, the latter the commentary upon that text. An analysis of the Talmud must therefore begin with that of the Mishna. By the term Mishna we designate a collection of decisions and traditional laws, embracing all departments of legislation, civil and religious. This code, which was the work of several generations of Rabbis, received its final redaction towards the end of the second century at the hands of Rabbi Jehuda the Holy. It is divided into six sections, which in turn are subdivided into treatises, chapters, and paragraphs. (The section is called Seder; the treatise, Massecheth, literally web; the chapter, Perek; the paragraph, the simplest element of the code, bears the name of the code itself, Mishna. The following summary of the contents of the six sections will enable the reader to appreciate the extended variety of the subjects embraced by the legislation of the Mishna.

Section I: Seeds- After a chapter devoted to the benedictions, it treats of tithes, first fruits, sacrifices, and gifts due from the produce of the land to the priests, the Levites, and

# THE TALMUD

the poor; of the cessation of agricultural labor during the Sabbatic year; and of the prohibited mixtures in seeds and in grafting- In all eleven treatises.

Section II: Feasts- Of the Sabbath and Sabbath rest, of feasts and fasts; Passover, Tabernacles, New Year, the Day of Atonement, and the Fasts ; of work forbidden, ceremonies to be observed, and sacrifices to be brought on those days- Twelve treatises.

Section III: Women- The legislation concerning marriage, divorce, the levirate marriage, and adultery; vows and the regulations for the Nazirite- Seven treatises.

Section IV: Fines- Civil legislation, besides a tractate on idolatry, and one called Aboth, consisting of a collection of the ethical sentences of the Rabbis. This section treats of commercial transactions, purchases, sales, mortgages, prescriptions, etc.; of legal procedure, of the organization of tribunals, of witnesses, oaths, etc- Ten treatises.

Section V: Sacred Things- The legislation concerning sacrifices, the first-born, clean and unclean animals; the description of Herod's Temple- Eleven treatises.

Section VI: Purifications- Laws concerning Levitical cleanness and uncleanness ; clean and unclean persons and things, objects capable of becoming unclean by contact. Purifications- Twelve treatises.)

Its language a Hebrew that has suffered a strong Chaldaic infusion, and has freely adopted Latin and especially Greek words, the Mishna is written in a simple style, so concise as sometimes to be obscure. Digressions are avoided, and the anecdotes met with here and there are introduced with the object

# THE TALMUD

of illuminating opinions with the light of facts. It is useless to dwell on the legislation of the Mishna, which has so often been expounded and analyzed, recently again in an article in the Quarterly Review (Emanuel Deutsch, The Talmud, Quarterly Review. October, 1867.), let us proceed at once to the Gemara. But a word must first be said concerning a collection called Tosiftha.

Rabbi Jehuda the Holy had not incorporated in the Mishna all the decisions of the Rabbis that had preceded him. A considerable number found no place in the code, either because in his eyes they were not vested with sufficient authority, or because they were useless repetitions of those published by him. Under the name Boraithoth (externae), the greater part of the excluded decisions were collected a little later in the order of the Mishna, with the same divisions and subdivisions, and gave rise to a new book, the Tosiftha, or addition. The Tosiftha, the work of the Babylonian schools, was compiled by R. Hyya and R. Oshaya, and presents the same external characteristics as the Mishna- the same language and the same style- but anecdotes form a far more considerable element. The Tosiftha and the Boraithoth incorporated neither in the Tosiftha nor in the Mishna are among the constituent elements of the Gemara.

This, then, brings us to the Gemara, the perpetual commentary following the Mishna in all its divisions and subdivisions. (Not in absolutely all. Certain parts of the Mishna lack their Gemara, either because the discussions relating to them were not committed to writing, or because, though edited, they have not reached us. Thus, in the first and in the last section, a single treatise has its commentary. In the fifth, that on sacred things, two treatises are bereft of their commentaries.) It has come down to us in two different forms or redactions. The one is the work of the Palestinian schools, and was drawn up at Tiberias in about 380; the other emanates from the Babylonian academies

# THE TALMUD

at Sora, Nehardea, and Pumbeditha, and was reduced to writing by R. Ashi and his disciple Rabina, receiving its final shape from R. Jose in about 500.

The Babylonian Gemara, improperly called the Babylonian Talmud, is clearer and more complete than the Palestinian Gemara, still more inaccurately called the Jerusalem Talmud. The former, therefore, was adopted by the synagogue, and the other, of higher importance to critical research by reason of its greater antiquity, was neglected by the Rabbis and the copyists of the middle ages, and has reached us in a much damaged condition and not without having lost many a page in its journey across the centuries. Unfortunately, too, there exists but one manuscript copy of the Jerusalem Talmud, that used for the *editio princeps*: no other manuscript by the aid of which its mutilated text might be corrected has been preserved. Its Babylonian rival has had a happier lot; manuscripts are not lacking, though for the most part fragmentary, and up to 1864 there had appeared forty-four editions of this Talmud, including the Mishna, the Gemara, and the commentaries, all paged alike, each edition numbering thousands of copies, each copy containing 2,947 leaves, divided up into twelve massive folios.

In the language of the Mishna the groundwork is Hebrew; of the Gemara the same cannot be said. Its language comes closer to the popular idiom, a sort of Aramean, more or less corrupt. However, specimens of the Hebrew of every age are met with, sometimes even of the classic Hebrew, according to the antiquity of the incorporated texts. After the return from the Captivity, Hebrew was an artificial language used by the Rabbis, degenerating little by little into low Hebrew, impregnating itself more and more with Aramaic elements, and finally merging into the dialect of the people. This explains how it happens that a single page of the Talmud contains three or four different languages, or rather specimens of one language at three or four

# THE TALMUD

different stages of degeneracy. It is not rare to find the redactor of the Talmud confirming the opinion of a Rabbi of the fourth century by quoting that of a teacher of the second, word for word the same as the former, except that it is written in Hebrew. The general principle may be enunciated, that purity of language is testimony to the antiquity of the texts reproduced in the Talmud.

Let us penetrate further into the Gemara, and consider its various features. The first striking characteristic is the extent of the commentary as compared with that of the text. Many a Mishna of five or six lines is accompanied by fifty or sixty pages of explanation. In so prolix an elaboration, of course, the lucid order of an adept's exposition must not be expected. The broad lines of a well defined plan providing a proper place for each part of the Gemara would be sought in vain. The modern scholar with his habits of order and method would find himself singularly out of his element there. Usually the Gemara presents the appearance of a boundless sea of discussions, digressions, narratives, legends, wherein the Mishna awaiting explanation is completely submerged. The reader of its pages, in which the most widely separated objects are as a matter of course placed in close juxtaposition, in which all things mix and clash with each other in the magnificence of barbaric disorder, might readily imagine himself a spectator at the enactment of an endless dream, subject to no laws but those of the association of ideas. Not even the most circumscribed discussions fail to give room to this characteristic disorder. For instance, to elucidate a point under discussion a quotation is needed- a quotation of a line. Let it not be supposed that it is considered sufficient to indicate the new argument incidentally. It is developed quite at length with all its ramifications, so that, to grasp its whole extent, it becomes necessary to forget the first and chief object that suggested it. Nor is this all.

This argument in turn calls up another, not in the least

germane to the principal question, and after the mind has been straying among unrelated digressions for the space of five or six pages, it must, in order to reach the starting point, painfully retrace the successive series of arguments, extricating as it goes along details useful in the discussion, if any there be. Worse still when the commentary by the essential nature of its object lacks stability and precision. In the explanation of a Mishna the opinion of a Rabbi is quoted; the Mishna is put aside in order to reproduce all the opinions bearing this Rabbi's name. Among them are moral dicta or principles of hygiene. In consequence, a whole page of maxims or of medical formulas defile before the reader. Then follow incantations, tales of demons, popular legends. Often the connecting link is not visible. Chance has brought together two absolutely irrelevant fragments- sufficient reason for the redactor of the Gemara to join them to each other. In this flood of digressions, the Mishna seems forgotten; the reader at all events has lost it from sight, so completely have his thoughts been borne away on this meandering course, directed, it seems, by fancy alone. But suddenly it meets his eye as at a turn in the road. The thread is resumed, the explanation proceeds. But how many digressions are needed to make a Mishna exhaust its Gemara!

"It is only after a time," says the author of the Quarterly Review article on the Talmud, "that the student learns to distinguish between two mighty currents in the book- currents that at times flow parallel, at times seem to work upon each other, and to impede each other's action; the one emanating from the brain, the other from the heart- the one prose, the other poetry- the one carrying with it all those mental faculties that manifest themselves in arguing, investigating, comparing, developing, bringing a thousand points to bear upon one and one upon a thousand; the other springing from the realms of fancy, of imagination, feeling, humor... The first named is called Halachah (Rule, Norm), a term applied both to the process of evolving

# THE TALMUD

legal enactments and the enactments themselves. The other, Haggadah (Legend, Saga), not so much in our modern sense of the word, though a great part of its contents comes under that head, but because it was only a 'saying,' a thing without authority..."

In fact, precise as are the boundaries of the domain of the Halacha, so vague and ill-defined are those of the Haggada. It is elusive, varying from the fantastic legend to the moral maxim, from the magic formula to historical narratives and chronological records. It is an accurate definition to say that it is what is not Halacha. The latter, on the other hand, is clearly defined; for everything called Halacha has a sacred character, compelling the respect of the believer. Halacha is LAW in all its authority; it constitutes dogma and cult, it is the fundamental element of the Talmud, and with it we ought to begin our investigation of the Gemara.

# THE TALMUD

## II: THE HALACHA

The name Halacha applies, not only to the special laws established by the Rabbis, but also to the discussions that result in the establishment of such laws. The schools did not stop at the text fixed by Rabbi Jehuda; they used it as the point of departure, and with the aid of various Boraithoth and the Tosiftha, they went on to explain and develop the Mishna and render new decisions. The Mishna, in fact, could not be considered a final text. When earlier decisions are adduced, it usually fails to indicate their source; sometimes the name of the author is added, but only in order to oppose another authority cited in the same way; and in the latter case, though sometimes a decision between the two antagonistic opinions is made, the question is most frequently left suspended. All this must be taken up again, the discussions begun must be finished, the points under debate determined with precision, order and light introduced everywhere: this is the work of the Gemara. It first devotes itself to the laws set down as established, inquires into their origin, and rejects the various explanations offered, until one is found holding its own against all objections. Often it shows that the decision reached by the Mishna is incomplete, obscure, contradictory, and that it cannot be made to apply to all the cases that ought apparently to come under it.

In other places the Gemara quotes against the Mishna a Tosiftha or a Boraltha of equal or of greater antiquity, one, therefore, invested with as much or with more authority. Thence arises a great variety of hypotheses; the discussions grow in extent and depth until an exhaustive explanation of the text is reached. Naturally, free play is granted to infinite variations in form. To give an accurate idea of the discussions would be difficult. It is preferable for us to venture upon a quotation, which will convey more than could be said about it. Opening at

# THE TALMUD

random a volume of the Talmud, we make choice of one example among a thousand. Here is what we read on folio 37b of the treatise Gittin, or Divorces:

> MISHNA: A slave taken captive and ransomed by a third party to be a slave, is a slave; ransomed to be set free, he cannot be made a slave. R. Simeon, son of Gamaliel, says that in any case he may be made a slave. (The above translation of the text being somewhat of a paraphrase, it seems to us of interest to give a Latin translation, whose absolute literalness is the excuse for its strange barbarity.)

> GEMARA: Of what case does the Mishna speak? Has he been ransomed by the third party before the first owner has renounced his right of possession? Ransomed to become free, why should he not be made a slave? Is it after that renunciation? Ransomed to be a slave, why should he not be free? Abaia answers: The Mishna should be explained thus; We are dealing with the case in which the first owner has not renounced his right, and the slave ransomed to remain a slave returns to serve his first master; ransomed to be free, he serves neither the second, who ransomed him to set him at liberty, nor the first, who might have permitted him to remain in captivity. R. Simeon, son of Gamaliel, says: In any case he remains the slave of the first master, because it is everybody's duty to ransom slaves equally with free men (and consequently it cannot be supposed that the first master would have allowed his slave to remain in captivity).

> Raba answers: This is the way to understand the Mishna: We are dealing with the case in which the first owner has renounced his right upon the slave. And the Mishna declares that, ransomed in order to remain a slave, the slave serves his second master; ransomed to be set free, he serves neither the first, who has renounced his right, nor the second, who ransoms him to set

# THE TALMUD

him at liberty. And R. Simeon, son of Gamaliel, says that in any case he remains a slave, because he admits Hiskia's principle, namely, that if liberty could be obtained thus, slaves would deliver themselves up to the enemy in the hope of being ransomed and becoming free.

But in a Boraitha it is said: R. Simeon, son of Gamaliel, says to the Rabbis: "As it is a duty to ransom free men, so it is a duty to ransom slaves." The explanation of the Mishna given by Abaia agrees with the Boraitha, since Abaia attributes to R. Simeon ben Gamaliel precisely this reason. But how can the Boraitha be understood in the explanation by Raba, since Raba can justify R. Simeon ben Gamaliel's opinion only by Hiskia's principle?

Raba answers: This Boraitha is incomplete, and itself needs the following interpretation: R.Simeon ben Gamaliel, not knowing the opinion of the Rabbis exactly, says to them: If you speak of the case in which the first master has not renounced his right, I admit the principle, "As it is a duty to ransom, etc." If of the opposite case, Hiskia's principle must be admitted. But how can Raba, who admits that the slave ransomed to be a slave belongs to him that has ransomed him, not to his first owner, who has renounced his rights- how can Raba justify the second owner's rights of possession? Through whom does he hold them? Through the captors who took the slave prisoner. But the captors themselves, whence do they derive their rights? Etc.

And the discussion on this Mishna of three lines continues for seven whole pages. It appears, from the above passage, that in its Halachic portions the Gemara uses the dialogue form. But it will not do to think of Plato's animated dialogues, in which the reader sees not only thoughts conflicting and clashing, but souls with their passions, their sentiments, with all that makes them human. Here we have dialectics in its driest

# THE TALMUD

and most laborious development. The disputants are not men, but names and arguments. And the style!- if the language in which the discussions are clothed can be dignified with the name style. At times the phraseology is diffuse, and, swathed in a score of words when six or eight would suffice, the idea drags painfully. Again, at other times, the language is exasperatingly concise, a letter standing for a word, a word for a clause. Questions whose complete statement would take lines are indicated by a single term, from which, as it were, they hang suspended. There are peculiar formulas in which whole ideas seem to have deposited themselves and become crystallized. The two words Alama thenan (verum cur docent) mean; "But if you maintain that only the thesis contrary to the one upheld by me is true, why is it taught?"- The word Minalan (unde nobis?), found at the beginning of a number of Gemaras, means: "What is the origin of the decision of the Mishna?" But as one Mishna ordinarily comprises several, only the answer and the objections made to the answer can clear up the thought. Suppress the commentary by Rashi, that masterpiece of precision and clearness, and the Talmud becomes almost enigmatic even to a proficient Talmudist. Put Buxtorf's Talmudic Dictionary (I do not mention a grammar; there exists none of the language of the Gemara) into the hands of a scholar that has a fair knowledge of Hebrew and Aramaic, but has never seen the Talmud; it will be impossible for him to decipher a page. We say decipher, and the figure of speech is not exaggerated; he truly has before him a text of hieroglyphs or inscriptions in unknown' characters. So true is this that even the Jews, who find the study of the Talmud easier than others, speak only of deciphering it. Suppose the teaching of the Talmud suddenly interrupted during the life of a generation; the tradition once lost, it would be well nigh impossible to recover it. The difficulties are of diverse kinds, growing out of the language and the subjects. The linguistic perplexities are certainly not lessened by the methods of teaching employed up to the present time. The inadequacy of the books compels the student to have recourse to the peculiar method of traditional teaching, that painful method which effects mastery of the language only by means of long habit. But a good grammar, a complete lexicon, a table of Talmudic formulas- they are not excessively numerous- would greatly curtail the labor. Yet, the greatest difficulties would remain to be conquered, difficulties almost insuperable, because inherent in the very nature of Talmudic argumentation. The lucid French mind would be hard put to it to reconcile itself to these discussions, which wind in and out through endless labyrinths of subtlest reasoning.

It were absolutely necessary to assume the Oriental habit of mind, that ease and force of imagination which bear thought beyond the limits of our systematic, straitlaced logic, and enable it to grasp the intangible relations between the most widely separated things. It is necessary to accustom oneself to that refinement of reasoning which penetrates to the innermost depths of an idea, and analyzes its most delicate, most evanescent shades, until the feeling of reality fades away. The influence such a book can wield upon the intelligence of a nation is patent. Th,e daily study of the Talmud, which among Jews began with the age of ten to end with life itself, necessarily was a severe gymnastic exercise for the mind, thanks to which it acquired incomparable subtlety and acumen.

Reasoning accustomed itself to accuracy, thinking to logic; in a word, intelligence grew in depth. In depth, mark you, not in extent. Discipline a well-endowed mind with Talmudic study, and you will produce a dialectician, forceful by reason of his logic and his penetration; you will have the unequaled scholars of the French, German, or Polish schools, who spend all their ability on casuistic commentaries; you will have a Spinoza, who carries Talmudic acuteness and profundity into philosophy. But do not expect to find largeness of view, breadth of outlook, expansiveness of ideas. The Halacha ignores all that. It is ratiocination, deductive reasoning raised to the highest power, and takes no account of inductive reasoning. This characteristic of the Halacha naturally suggests another monument raised by learned men to the glory of religion, and one is tempted to pronounce the name of Scholasticism. In fact, the comparison is seductive. Scholasticism, like the Halacha, is the work of schools; like the Halacha, it rests upon deduction; and like it, employs the deductive method. But though Scholasticism with the Syllogism, and the Talmud with its hermeneutic laws, with the seven rules of Hillel, with R. Ishmael's thirteen principles, or Akiba's method, seek to do but one thing, namely, to demonstrate, they differ absolutely as to the aim of their demonstrations. The one wishes by reasoning to establish the reality of dogmatic principles; the other tries only to remember, to recall half forgotten or badly reported legal decisions, and, by an effort of reasoning memory, to rediscover them in their entirety.

Scholasticism is a philosophic system, very limited, to be sure, very petty, an enslaved system, *ancilla theologiae*; but as human reason is not called upon to do its full part, this philosophy will some day dominate and overthrow theology. Talmudic Halacha is anything but this. Philosophy it knows not even by name, and cannot know it; moreover, it ought not to know it, since it aspires to but one thing; to establish for Judaism a *Corpus Juris Ecclesiastici*.

If the nature of the Halacha has been made clear, and if besides it is remembered that it embraces all departments of religious and civil legislation, it will be seen how limited a construction must be put upon the word encyclopedia, which has been freely applied to the Talmud. The Talmud is indeed an encyclopedia in the sense that it contains information on all subjects of knowledge cultivated in the epoch of its composition, all of which have left in it some trace or reminder of themselves.

# THE TALMUD

But one must not expect to see the Rabbis treat the sciences as such. Cast a glance at the summary of the contents of the Mishna given at the beginning of this article. The first section deals with the laws having reference to the products of the field. Some among them bear on the mixing of seeds. Thus the Rabbis are led to speak incidentally of botany and to adduce certain botanic facts previously acquired with the sole aim of making them subserve the establishment of the Halacha. The second section treats of the Sabbath and the feasts. With regard to the Sabbath, one of the great questions is that of Sabbath repose.

It is prohibited to go beyond a radius of two thousand steps from one's house on that day. But in order, to determine the limits in despite of the accidents of the ground, of valleys, hills, watercourses, certain geometric facts must be considered, and hence our Rabbis are obliged to talk geodesy. The fixing of the dates of the festivals presupposes that of a calendar, which again requires astronomical knowledge. Hence our doctors now turn to astronomy, and demand of her guidance in the establishment of the legislation for the feasts. Elsewhere, the discussion turns on prohibited animal food. Meat is forbidden when derived from animals presenting specific characteristics that render them unclean, or from clean animals tainted by certain diseases causing their prohibition. To determine these specific characteristics or these morbid conditions, some knowledge of anatomy and physiology is necessary.

This part of Halachic legislation, then, displays the results of natural history studies without permitting the assertion that natural history is specifically treated. Finally, in another place, in the laws on the causes of uncleanness in persons (issues, menses, etc.), the lawmakers take up physiology and medicine, inasmuch as they apply to religious legislation the results of physiologic and medical observation. Thus the Rabbis are led to speak of all the departments of knowledge . cultivated

# THE TALMUD

in their time, in order to abstract from them principles available for the establishment of the Halachoth. Moreover, this miscellaneous knowledge was acquired, not for its own sake, but to press it into the service of the Halacha. Science was not the end, merely the instrument permitting the attainment of the end.

Nevertheless it took protracted study to compass the Halacha in all its extent and diversified manifestations. The title of Rabbi was not to be gained in a few years, and at a period in which books were rare, in which, particularly, tradition might not be reduced to writing, a long pupilage was necessary to entitle one to participation in the discussions of the sages. One is almost tempted to take literally the Talmudic accounts that tell of twenty years passed by some of the eminent doctors of the Halacha in the apprenticeship to the Law. To complete our examination of the various characteristics of the Halacha, the method of instruction remains to be considered. The Rabbis kept schools (Beth ha-Midrash, house of study) in the localities in which they lived, and numerous disciples gathered in them. Some doctrinal point was assigned to the students for elaboration, and on the day of the discussion they presented themselves with their arguments all prepared. The master catechized them, and by a series of questions skilfully put led them to find the answers themselves.

The instruction, then, was not technically such; it was a protracted conversation into which the Rabbis decoyed their disciples, and from which they boasted that they derived as much profit as the latter. The disciples, in turn, spread the doctrine of their master abroad. Thence the expression met with at every step in the Talmud: "Such a one says in the name of so-and-so, who had it from such another." As for the discussions that were to result in the fixation of the Law, they took place in the following way. The Rabbis met in the tribunal or Sanhedrin, often accompanied by their pupils, who listened in silence behind a bar. After a public discussion, the point of doctrine was decided by a plurality of the votes of the Rabbis. The session was presided over by the Nassi, or prince, and by the president of the tribunal (Ab Beth Din, the chief of the house of justice), the two religious heads of the nation. The Talmud asserts that these two dignities date back to the institution of the Great Synagogue, and perpetuated themselves without interruption from Simeon the Just, contemporary of Alexander the Great and last member of that assembly. Then Mishna cites a series of couples (zugoth) of Rabbis succeeding each other in the instruction of the oral Law from Simeon the Just to Hillel and Shammai, and seems to confer the title of Nassi on the first, and Ab Beth Din on the second, of each couple. Hillel and Shammai were the last of the series of couples, and their successors explicitly bear the two titles. As instruction was obligatory and schools were numerous in Palestine, every man, no matter of what rank, could aspire to the highest dignities. Outside of the priesthood, knowledge alone constituted nobility. Witness Akiba, who from the estate of a simple shepherd rose to be the great doctor of the Mishna, 'the second Moses.' The Talmud Chacham (student), if he distinguished himself, received the title of doctor from his masters, and though gratitude and the admiration of the public reserved the title of Nassi for the illustrious family of Hillel, at least the Rabbis could choose the Ab Beth Din from among those most deserving of the office. When the student was. judged worthy of the title of doctor. Rabbinical authority was conferred upon him by a peculiar ceremony called Semicha or Imposition (of the hands). This ordination was absolutely necessary to give him the right to decide and to forbid, to invest him actually with the power to which his knowledge entitled him morally. The ceremony was of the utmost importance for the Jews, since it was efficacious in insuring the perpetuity of tradition, as was well illustrated during the persecutions of Hadrian, at the time of Bar-Cochba's revolt. Wishing to destroy the Jewish nation, Hadrian condemned to death every Rabbi convicted of having given or received the Semicha. "One day," the Talmud tells, "a

# THE TALMUD

government decree condemned to the rack both him that gave and him that received the Semicha. The city in which the ceremony took place with its environs in a radius of two thousand steps, was to be destroyed. What did Judah ben Baba do? He placed himself in a valley between two large towns, Usha and Shepharam, and ordained five disciples, R. Mefr, R. Judah, R. Simeon, R. Jose, and R. Nehemiah. Scarcely was the ceremony completed when the enemy perceived them. R. Judah ben Baba had time only to say to the Rabbis: 'Flee, my sons!'- 'And thou, O master?', 'I am like a stone that lies immovable.' And it is said that the Roman soldiers did not abandon his body until they had riddled it like a sieve with three hundred lance-thrusts." Later, when the right of Semicha was irrevocably taken from the Jews of Palestine, the work of the schools stopped, and the chain of tradition was broken. The constantly growing power of the Church thus led to the closing of the Bathe-Midrashim, and in about 370 the critical condition of the school of Tiberias forced the Rabbis to reduce to writing the Palestinian Gemara ( Talmud Jerushalmi).

# THE TALMUD

## III: THE HAGGADA

We have now arrived at the second current whose existence in the 'sea of the Talmud,' to employ the expression of the Rabbis, was mentioned above. The question. What is the Haggada, we answered by saying that whatever in the Talmud does not appertain to the legal discussions, and does not bear upon the explanation of the Halacha, belongs to the realm of the Haggada. It embraces not only homilies, preaching, and edifying explanations of the Bible- all that addresses itself to the heart to touch it, to the mind to persuade it- but also history and legend, the most varied information of a scientific character in mathematics, astronomy, physics, medicine, and natural history. The Haggada is talk in all its wide play and vague generality, the daily on *dit*, simple conversation or moral instruction, interrupting or following the learned and painful discussions of the school and resting the weary spirit. It is evident, then, that the Haggada cannot have authority, and though it may elicit veneration from the crowd, because it issues from the mouth of official teachers whose words are respected, its characteristic is not legality; it does not legislate. "Objections are not raised to a Haggada," is one of the rules of the Talmud. Elsewhere it is said, "A decision is not rendered according to the Haggada." The Rabbis specially devoted to the study of the Halacha, maliciously applying to the Aggadist a verse from Ecclesiastes, called him, A man to whom God hath given riches, yet giveth him not power to enjoy them, because "he can make use of his Haggadistic knowledge neither to permit nor to forbid, neither to declare clean nor to declare unclean." In the immense field of the Haggada the Oriental mind unfolds in all its wealth and fullness. Here especially we must seek the beliefs, ideas, sentiments that animated the Jewish, indeed the Asiatic world, in the productive centuries that saw the enormous expansion of the superstitions of the Empire and the germination and growth of the religion of

# THE TALMUD

Jesus and the apostles; that saw the rich development of Oriental mysticism and the supreme effort of Greek philosophy shedding a last and brilliant gleam. This treasury, where the noblest beliefs the world has been able to conceive, as well as the most fantastic thoughts that have ever crossed human brain, lie promiscuously heaped up, is a sort of microcosm, in which that submerged civilization reappears in its most salient features. Add all that is characteristic of Judaism, and gives it its distinctive stamp- its religious and moral beliefs, its customs and usages springing from its religious doctrines, or, if borrowed from neighboring nations, so completely transformed and so well marked by the Jewish impress as to appear Jewish- and you will understand the profound charm exercised by the Haggada over the thinker and the scholar that investigate the manifestations of human thought under whatever form they appear. A great piece of work might be done- the sifting and coordinating of the Haggada's heterogeneous wealth. It would be necessary to go over the whole ground, and make a systematic classification, such as we of modern times demand; show what the Haggada knew of the exact and what of the natural sciences; present the allotment of truths which it has been able to discover and of errors which it harbors. It would be necessary to scrutinize its morality and its religious philosophy (the only philosophy it knows), and see to what level it was able to rise. And it were specially important to study the oddities, the fables, the superstitions of the Haggada, since in the history of the human mind nothing is more instructive than the study of the diseases of the intellect, which enable us the better to understand the mind in its healthy state, on the principle that sends physiology to the examination of morbid phenomena. The stranger the customs of other nations appear to us, the odder their manner of feeling and of regarding things, the more fruitful a source are observation and research for the philosopher.

Nothing, therefore, may be neglected, and without

# THE TALMUD

fearing the outrage to our habits or the shock to our modern taste, we should accept the pebble as well as the precious stone, mud and slime as well as the pure and limpid waters; in a Word, bring together all the productions of the popular imagination, whatever they may be, in which nature expresses herself in all her naivete, and displays herself in her nakedness. This is the work, not without dignity and charm, that awaits performance, and that might tempt a mind at once patient and bold. But it is easy enough to trace out a plan or point out a desideratum. The important thing is to realize both. We make no pretense of giving even a sketch of the work indicated. We content ourselves with putting together some few features that convey at least an idea of the Haggada.

In the exact sciences, the Haggada presents the singular characteristic of a mixture of truths and errors, thus seeming to prove the acceptance of certain scientific traditions from alien sources rather than the existence of a method of investigation. Everywhere in the Talmud the ratio of the circumference to the diameter is as three to one, although four or five centuries earlier Archimedes had found it to be 22/7. The method indicated by the Mishna for measuring the width of a hill is most primitive. Two men measure it with a chain about four cubits in length, one of them holding one end against his stomach, the other holding the other end with his feet. The Talmud says; "The circumference of the world (that is, the length of the orbit described by the sun in his course from rising to setting) is about six thousand Peras, and the thickness of the firmament (that is, the distance from the sun to the earth) is about one thousand Peras." The first of these statements is an old tradition; the second is an inference from R. Jochanan's saying: A man walking at the ordinary pace can take thirty thousand steps a day, five thousand from the beginning of dawn to the first rays of the sun, and five thousand from sunset to the appearance of the stars. Thus the time taken by the sun to send us his light, namely, the period of the five thousand steps during dawn or twilight, is the sixth part of that devoted to the illumination of the world, the period of the thirty thousand steps. Then the thickness of the firmament is one-sixth of the length of the solar orbit. By the side of such puerilities, statements like the following are found: R. Gamaliel says; "There is a tradition in my grandfather's family that the new moon sometimes is ahead of her time, sometimes is delayed; in no case does she appear before the lapse of 29 ½ days plus 2/3 and 73 parts of an hour." The hour in the Talmud is divided into 1080 parts- in passing, notice the happy choice of a number divisible by every digit except 7. All reductions being made, we have 29 days, 12 hours, 44 minutes, 3.3+ seconds. The mean length of a synodic revolution being 29 days, 12 hours, 44 minutes, 2.8 seconds, the approximation is seen to be very close. Here is a curious assertion; "The sages of Israel maintain that the sphere is motionless, and that it is the planets that move; the learned men of other nations maintain that the planets are fixed to the sphere, which turns." But what is one to say about the following; "The sages of Israel maintain that during the day the sun rolls under the firmament, and during the night above it (which renders him invisible); the sages of other nations maintain the contrary." It seems that R. Joshua (towards the end of the first century) knew how to calculate the period of the comet to which Halley's name is attached. The Talmud speaks of the profound astronomical learning of Samuel the Babylonian, who made a special study of the moon. He is the one who asserted that he was as well acquainted with the paths of the heavenly bodies as with the streets of Nehardea; but he was wholly unable to explain the nature of comets. "We know only by tradition," he added, "that the comets do not cross Orion, else they would shatter the world, and if they appear to cross it, it is the light they cast that traverses the constellation, not they themselves." These quotations, in which the word tradition occurs several times, seem to prove that, though some of the Rabbis devoted themselves specially to the exact sciences, the others were totally unacquainted with them. Had they a scientific method of research? We do not think so; we rather incline to the opinion that the greater part of these scientific facts were borrowed either from the inhabitants of Irak or from the Greeks. In natural history and in anatomy the Haggada is clearer. Here the Rabbis made observations, doubtless because the Halacha is more particularly interested in these departments, having, for instance, to legislate on agricultural subjects, classify the mammals, the fish, and the birds as clean and unclean, and study the diverse diseases that can attack the clean animals. Therefore, facts were collected, animals dissected, their organs studied; the brain, whose superior and inferior membrane are known; the cerebellum, whose diseases may cause impotence; the spinal cord, which is the prolongation of the cerebellum, and whose lesions in certain cases are fatal, in others do not bring on death; the heart, with its two ventricles, its two auricles, and the pericardium.

The lungs and the stomach are the objects of special study. By the side of ingenious observations, general principles are found; "Every horned animal is clovenfooted.", "The presence of scales proves the existence of fins." The form of the egg indicates the class of the bird. The Rabbis observed that the milk of an unclean animal does not curdle; that animals cast their young by day or by night, according as they copulate by day or by night; that the union of animals with the same mode of copulation and the same period of pregnancy is fruitful. They know the amianthus that whitens in the fire. But they assert, agreeing in this respect with Lucretius, Pliny, and the whole ancient world, that the lion is afraid of the crowing of the cock; nor do they contradict another of Pliny's statements, that the salamander extinguishes fire. They look upon apes of the larger kinds as half men, and they know the Shamir, created, says the Mishna, during the twilight of the sixth day, a worm as large as a barley grain, whose look cleaves rocks; therefore, as the Temple

# THE TALMUD

was to be constructed with stones untouched by iron, the Shamir was used to cut them.

Natural history leads us to medicine, which was always cultivated among the Jews, and remained a scientific tradition with them up to modern times. It is, therefore, not surprising to find fairly extended information on the subject in the Haggada. Whole pages are taken up with the explanation of medical formulas and pharmaceutic prescriptions. There are hygienic lessons and series of injunctions as to the use of simples. Our ignorance of these matters forbids our making a selection and giving extracts. We believe, however, that it would be interesting to investigate whether the Haggada contains a collection of personal observations and true experiments, as they were considered to be by the Jewish scholars of the middle ages. The author of the Cozari, Jehuda Halevi, maintains that the Talmud boasts knowledge not to be found in either Aristotle or Galen. Perhaps, too, its notions are connected by general systematic views, in which case it would be necessary to investigate whether the medical theories were not borrowed from, or at least influenced by, the schools of Hippocrates, Galen, and Soranus. At all events, in our opinion, we have here an interesting problem in the history of medicine.

Did the Rabbis look with favor upon magical medicine, that mass of superstitious practices with which Chaldea flooded Asia and Europe. Knowing their disposition to be what it is, we can boldly answer. No. Somewhere in the Talmud it is told that King Hezekiah hid and destroyed a medical book, and the act is praised, because, says Maimonides, the book contained talismanic remedies. It is, nevertheless, not astonishing to find a large part of the Haggada given over to magic. Yet among the masters of the black art figures neither Samuel the Babylonian nor Theodosius the Palestinian, of whose medical science the Talmud imakes boast. There are Rabbis that recall with more or less credulity the popular superstitions, the study of which, it must be conceded, is not without interest, for it is very curious to see how pseudo-medical practices, common to the whole of Asia, among the Jews take on forms in which their peculiar genius is revealed. According to Pliny, the quartian fever is cured by suspending from one's neck the longest tooth of a black dog, or some dust in which a sparrow has wallowed, tied up in a piece of linen attached by a red thread. R. Huna is more exacting; "One must take seven thorns from seven palm trees, seven splinters from seven beams, seven pegs from seven bridges, seven cinders from seven ovens, seven grains of dust from seven door pivots, seven kinds of pitch from seven ships, seven caraway seeds, and, finally, seven hairs from seven old dogs." You recognize, do you not, in the multiplication of ingredients, the riotous imagination of the Oriental, and in the use of seven the Jewish tendency to make this number sacred. Perhaps, however, it is proper to look upon this prescription by R. Huna as hidden irony against the popular prejudices, which he is secretly combating even while appearing to lower himself to them. The following advice is characteristic, and leaves no room for uncertain interpretations; "Against a burning fever," says R. Jochanan, "take a knife made entirely of iron, go into the underbrush and tie a white hair to it; on the first day cut a notch into a thorn while saying the verse from Exodus: 'The angel of the Lord appeared unto Moses,' etc. (in the burning bush). The next day make another incision in the thorn, and say: 'The Lord saw that Moses turned aside to see.' The third day return, and say: 'God said to Moses, Draw not nigh hither.' That done, bend to the ground, and pronounce these words: 'Bush! Bush! it is not because thou art the greatest, but because thou art the humblest of the trees that the Holy One, blessed be He, has made His glory to descend upon thee, and as the fire was lighted before Hanania, Mishael, and Azaria, and fled before them, so may the fever which burns in me flee before me!'"

# THE TALMUD

If this practice was inspired by alien customs, Judaism has transformed it in a singular way, and given it its own impress. Means are found of turning popular superstitions to edifying uses and of reading an elevated lesson of morality into a good wife's prescription. Elsewhere Abala reports numerous formulas in the name of his mother, a woman celebrated in Talmudic demonology; three madder-colored threads (the red thread of Pliny?) around one's neck arrest disease, five drive it away, seven are a safeguard against spells- "Yes," says R. Aha bar Jacob, "if the wearer of the threads sees neither the sun, nor the moon, nor rain, and hears nor the noise of iron, nor that of the forge, nor the crowing of a cock.". "Why, then, the virtues of thy madder-colored threads fall to the ground," answers R. Nachman, "for thou demandest the impossible."

Turn a page, and from magic receipts we pass to pure magic. The Haggada unveils strange mysteries. It tells at great length of demons, who like mortals eat and drink, live and die, and reproduce themselves, in these respects partaking of human weakness, but who are winged, transport themselves in an instant over the whole universe, know the future, and invisible can assume any form they please. You are informed that some are charged with the mission of rubbing up against you without your knowledge, and that is the reason your garments wear out; that others delight in destroying unoccupied dwellings, but leave them at the sight of a man. Therefore, the owner of a deserted house ought to be grateful to him who takes up his residence in it. Some perch on the roofs, and are on the lookout for passers-by to cast a spell on them; others sit down on the parings of nails incautiously thrown on the ground; then woe to the woman with child who walks over them; others on onions, or on garlic with the outside skin taken off: beware of swallowing them along with those vegetables! Others hide themselves in water during the night; therefore, precautions must be taken when one is thirsty at night! Thus: "Do not drink at night. The demon

# THE TALMUD

Shabriri, who takes up his abode in water, is to be feared; he strikes blind those who drink. If, however, you are thirsty, awaken your companion, and say; Let us drink together. The demon will keep himself quiet. If you are alone, make a noise with your pillow, and say aloud, Thou so-and-so, son of so-and-so, thy mother has told thee: Beware of Shabriri, briri, riri, iri, ri, i, in white vases."

We might continue our quotations endlessly. The reader sees a phantasmagoria pass before his eyes, sometimes strange, odd, ridiculous, sometimes impish, bold, audacious, seeming to mock at the laws of nature and bid defiance to the rules of good sense or taste. Under the conjuring wand of the Haggada, new life animates the universe. The human soul seems to have transfused nature with her sentiments, her passions, her language. Trees, animals, stones are endowed with speech. The souls of the dead converse with one another in the graveyards. The infinitely great and the infinitely small are intermingled and confounded; by the side of the Shmnir, the marvelous worm whose look cleaves rocks, are gigantic monsters: the Behemoth, which every day browses on the grass of a thousand mountains, but which God castrated that its progeny might not destroy the whole of terrestrial vegetation; and the Leviathan, whose female, killed from a similar precaution, girdles the earth with her carcass. It is the unrolling of a vast fairy world, in which reason must perforce yield to riotous imagination. Who shall tell the history of these poetic or singular legends and their successive transformations in Mahomeddan and Christian mythology? Who shall tell the history of the tales of Asmodeus, Lilith, Sammael, originating doubtless in the depths of Chaldea and preserved by pious tradition throughout the centuries up to our day? Go to the remote parts of Alsace, or to Germany, or Poland; enter Jewish homes in which old customs have scarcely been encroached upon by modern civilization, and there, in the intimate intercourse of winter evenings, some good wife will tell you with pious terror the fantastic tales that mayhaps her captive ancestors heard two thousand years ago on the banks of the Euphrates.

Between legend and history the boundary line is not well marked, especially not in the imagination of an Oriental. Let us cross it, and inquire into the value of the Haggada as an historic authority. This question admits of two contradictory answers, for, according to the point of view, it is equally just to concede and to refuse value to it. To hope to find in the Haggada precise and detailed chronicles, scrupulously exact and circumstantial narratives of events, is to run the risk of complete disappointment. The Haggada is totally ignorant of what is properly called history. Reality and dream mingle in nebulous vagueness. It does not seem to have an accurate idea of time. The Orient, in fact, immobile in its unchangeable existence, cannot have the precise notion of time so clearly conveyed to the Occidental mind by perpetual mutations. Thus the various epochs of the past seem to be put upon the same plane. Edom, Nebuchadnezzar, Vespasian, Titus, Hadrian, all the enemies of the Jewish race, merge into one type, and one is substituted for the other in the long martyrology of its history. If, for instance, there is any event that should have left deep traces in the memory of the nation, it assuredly is the destruction of Jerusalem and the 'Holy House.'

Yet, concerning the various phases of the struggle, the men that took part in and directed it, and the final catastrophe, clear and accurate data are sought in vain. Aside from some vague details, in which the element of truth they may contain waits to be set free by criticism, absolutely nothing can be found. But what the Haggada does know, are the poetic legends that thrill the populace, and go straight to one's heart. It tells the story of Martha, the wife of the high priest Joshua ben Gamala, the elegant, fastidious lady to whom were applied the words of Deuteronomy: "The tender and delicate woman among you,

## THE TALMUD

which would not adventure to set the sole of her foot upon the ground for delicateness and tenderness," and who dies of hunger in the streets of Jerusalem, or, according to another version, is dragged across country bound by her hair to the tail of a wild horse. It tells the story of that Zadok who bewails the misery of his land, and in his grief condemns himself to a forty years' fast. "He ate only one fig a day, and he grew so thin that this fig could be seen to pass down his throat." It recounts with all possible precision the fortunes of the son and the daughter of the high priest Ishmael ben Elisha after the sack of the Holy City. They were sold as slaves to two neighboring masters- Said the first, I have a slave of incomparable beauty- And I, said the other, possess the most beautiful maiden imaginable. Let us join them in marriage, and share their children- In the evening they locked them up together in a chamber. The youth remained in one corner, the maiden in another. The former said: I, a priest, the son of a high priest, should take to wife a slave! The latter said: I, the daughter of a high priest, should marry a slave! Thus they lamented all night. With the dawn came recognition, and each leaping towards the other, they stood clasped in close embrace until their souls took flight. And, stirred to his depths, the narrator, recalling the verse in Lamentations, exclaims, "For these things I weep; mine eye, mine eye runneth down with water."- Such are the recollections that remain of the catastrophe- legends and tales. This is no longer history, or, if you will, it is still history, but of the kind made by the people.

Assuredly, it will not do to require of the Haggada the exactitude of an historic chronicle. And if perchance we find here and there, buried under a thick layer, a few precise data, a few accurate notes, a few lines of history, the Seder Olam (Chronicle of the World), the Megillath Taanith (Roll of Fasts), it must nevertheless be conceded that the Haggada has nearly no value at all as a documentary source. But precisely because the narrative of facts is merged into legend, the Haggada ought to

# THE TALMUD

yield all the interest of legendary chronicles. It will not do to turn up one's nose at legend ; it is the absolutely necessary complement of history, which usually presents facts in all their nudity and dryness. But facts are far from being all that is essential. There is the idea hiding beneath the facts and dominating them, as vital force animates the skeleton of an animal. Now this idea, which only with great difficulty can be abstracted from a series of facts, appears in all its clearness in legend. By means of legends, a people expresses its desires, its aspirations, its ideal, later translated into facts, and expresses them with precision so much the greater as the form of the legend is vague and its web loose. In legend we have first a narrative, in itself without historic value, and then the idea, which is crystallized in the narrative form, and which answers to a real sentiment, reproduced with the greatest clearness, and therefore of considerable value to the historian. In this sense legend should be invested with authority of a certain kind, and this is the authority that the Haggada may lay claim to. In the Haggada, we find local color; it conveys Jewish manners, customs, and beliefs, the spirit of the institutions and the religion, in a word, the soul and the life of the nation.

To complete this all too superficial examination of the Haggada, there remains for us to speak of its moral and religious philosophy. The Quarterly Review writer, with the warmth characteristic of his fine plea for the Talmud, has given an eloquent exposition of the system, reproducing Abraham Nager's substantial contribution to the subject. We shall give a resume of the same work, supplying certain features that were omitted and that to us appear important. In the beginning there was nothing. God, by an act of His will, created matter or the first substance, according to some, water, according to others, water, air, and fire, and organizing these elements. He formed, 'in His own good time,' the world as it is. God, then, is at once 'creator and architect.'- What was the process of creation. That is a mystery.

# THE TALMUD

Certain it is that the angels had naught to do with it, for they were formed at the earliest on the second day of creation, 'that it might not be said: Michael stretched out the firmament to the north, and Gabriel to the south.' But the world once created, Providence brought nothing to pass 'without consulting the celestial household.' Besides, there is an angel, 'the master of the world,' who is the intermediary between heaven and earth, Metatron, that is, the one seated near the heavenly throne (metatronos). Each nation, nevertheless, has its special tutelary angel, as well as its guardian constellations, with the exception of Israel, who has 'neither angel nor constellation, so long as he observes the divine law.' Israel stands under the eye of God Himself.

At the same time with the world, God created miracles, which thenceforth fall under the immutable laws of nature regulating the universe despite the evil that may result. Creation has for its end man, who in turn is to use the world to execute the will of God on earth, the aim of creation thus being the realization of the divine here below. 'If Israel accepts the Law (all other nations having refused it), God will maintain the world; if not, He will cause it to drop back into nothingness.' The aim of man on earth, then, is the knowledge and the practice of the Law, 'without which there were neither heaven nor earth'- the Law 'on which God had His eye fixed when He created the universe, as the mason that builds a house has in mind the plans and the external appearance.'

Man endowed with free will, 'created last on the eve of the Sabbath, that he might at once take his place at the holy banquet,' ought therefore to strive endlessly for perfection, which eventually renders him superior to the angels, for, in spite of their eternal and infinite perfection, they are without liberty, and neither earn commendation nor incur censure. How is this perfection reached? By the practice of the Law and the doing of

# THE TALMUD

good deeds. Useless to give examples of the morality of the Pharisees. The subject is too familiar. It is well known that the Talmud may lay claim to the most exalted ideals of goodness that human mind can conceive of, and that all the moral ideas incorporated in the Gospels had long before passed from mouth to mouth in the streets of Jerusalem. Glance through the Mishnic treatise Aboth, and you will find all that the most delicate charity, the most refined and intelligent kindliness can inspire into souls naturally disposed to the good. Human dignity, the sacredness of manual labor, the superiority of good works over learning, the equality of men before the divine tribunal, no matter what religion they may profess- these are the great principles asserted and preached by the Haggada on every page.

The Talmud, says Nager, has its peculiar psychology. In a number of passages the Platonic theory of the pre-existence of souls is stated, but nowhere does metempsychosis appear. Plato's doctrine appealed to the poetic imagination of the Rabbis more than the Aristotelian theory, which made of the soul the entelechy of the body. All the souls called to terrestrial life were created in the beginning, and kept in reserve. They have all-embracing knowledge of the Law up to the moment in which they unite with a body. Then an angel closes the mouth of the child, and the soul forgets all it knew- No original sin; "As God is pure, so the soul is pure."- Every child on leaving its mother's womb is made to swear by an angel that it will be just. "Be assured," he says to it, "that God is pure, that His servants are pure, and that the soul given to thee is also pure." In one passage, however, a teacher speaks of the crime of Adam, which recoils on the whole of mankind. "When the serpent tempted Eve", it corrupted her with its venom. Israel, by being witness of the Revelation at Sinai, was cured of the disease; "the idolaters could not be cured." But in general the story of the first sin has not found an echo in the teachings of the sages. Elsewhere it is expressly said; "No death without sin, no grief without fault." It

# THE TALMUD

is also said that children dying in infancy or at birth may enter into the future life.

Whence, then, comes sin? From man's free will. "Everything is foreseen," says Akiba, "but liberty is granted." And elsewhere; "Everything is in the power of God except the fear of God." Human destiny is not fulfilled here below; the other world is the soul's true home. This earth is but "the caravansary by the wayside," in which a brief rest is taken. The dogmas of the immortality of the soul and a future life are energetically asserted by the Rabbis, who regard their negation as veritable heresy. But how is one to understand the entrance into the future life? Do you understand the entrance into this life. Death and birth resemble each other, say the Rabbis. Suppose a child in its mother's womb to know that after the lapse of a few months it will leave the place it occupies. That would seem to it the most grievous event that could happen. It is so comfortable in the element that surrounds it, and protects it against outside influences. However, the time of separation approaches; with terror it sees the protecting envelopes torn asunder, and it believes that the hour of death has arrived. But the moment of leaving its little world marks the beginning of a nobler, more beautiful, more perfect life, which lasts until a voice again sounds at its ear proclaiming : Thou must leave earth, as thou didst leave thy mother's womb, and, stripping off this earthly vesture, thou must once more die, once more begin life.

A new life opens for man, a life wholly spiritual, in which he receives the recompense or the chastisement for his conduct here below. "In the world to come, there is neither eating, nor drinking, nor any material pleasure; but the just sit there with crowns on their heads, and delight in the glory of the Divine Presence."- "The souls of the just, at the foot of the celestial throne, contemplate the splendor of God." Those of the impious are condemned to the torments of the nether world.

# THE TALMUD

Eternal punishment is reserved for well defined classes of sinners, as, for example, those who knowing the Law have entirely abjured it, and those who not only sin themselves, but draw others into crime. The description of these tortures is vague and contradictory, as is that of the lower regions themselves. In fact, the Talmud gives us, not so much a system, as a series of individual opinions.

The fire in the Valley of Hinnom (Ge-Hinnom, gehenne) plays the principal role. As the Rabbis incline more or less to the popular beliefs, the descriptions are more or less material. The same holds good in the descriptions of future rewards. For instance, we have the peculiar belief that the flesh of the Leviathan, preserved in salt since the first days of creation, will be divided among the just, and that from its tanned hide tents will be made whose brilliancy will fill the universe. Such fantastic features, equally characteristic of the hell and the paradise of the middle ages, do not affect the elevated spirituality pervading these beliefs. Thus we have one Rabbi denying the very existence of hell. "There is no hell in the future world" says R. Simon ben Lakish. "But the Most Holy makes to shine His sun, whose splendor fills the righteous with happiness, and causes the wicked to suffer." Thus the soul finds reward or punishment within itself. The student recognizes, to use the expression of the schools, the subjective character of the sanction attached to the moral law. Such are the teachings transmitted by the Haggada, and spread among the people by popular preaching. They were conveyed in a peculiar and rather original form well worthy of description.

All of them were connected with the Bible, to which the Rabbis considered themselves obliged to trace the ideas they developed. It is the application to the Haggada of the method created by R. Akiba for the Halacha. The orator took a verse, which he commented on in a thousand ingenious ways, deducing

# THE TALMUD

from it all sorts of moral lessons. It mattered little to him, if he did violence to the words, or abused a grammatical construction, or changed letters or words according to his caprice.

Equally little it concerned his listeners, who, however, were not deceived, knowing as well as himself the fantastic character of his explanations. But nothing equals the ease with which they accepted them, for they craved only edification. Yet the preacher called to his aid allegory, parable, legend, which accompanied the commentary on the text, and sometimes even were confused with it. And as he had the powerful and facile imagination of the Oriental, he needed only the gift of fluent speech to charm an audience disposed to yield to his fascinations, convinced in advance, and happy to hear another give utterance to the feelings hidden in their hearts. The orator might be one of the doctors of the Halacha that addressed the congregations assembled in the synagogues on days of reunion, Sabbaths or holidays. In such cases true homilies were pronounced. But usually the speaker was any chance person that gathered a crowd about him on the street, and held it under the spell of his improvisations. Such were Judah, the son of Seripheus, and Matathias, the son of Margaloth, those victims of Herod of whom Josephus speaks, those beloved orators endowed with the gift of inspiring crowds and enkindling popular risings. "Who wishes to live, to live long," cries an Aggadist in the open street. 'Who wishes to buy happiness?' The original questions attract a crowd demanding to know the orator's secret. "Thou desirest to live many days," he answers, "thou wishest to enjoy peace and happiness? Keep thy tongue from evil, and thy lips from speaking guile. Seek peace, and pursue it. Depart from the evil, and do good." And paraphrasing these words of the Psalmist (Ps. xxxiv, 13- IS), he develops his ideas in the midst of the attentive crowd.

What, in fact, was the importance of Aggadistic

# THE TALMUD

teaching? Assuredly it had considerable value. The study of the Halacha could have appealed only to a restricted part of the Jewish population. The schools and the academies doubtless were frequented by a large number of disciples, eager to listen to the instruction of the Rabbis. But they by no means constituted the kernel of the population, and what was there for the people outside of this popular preaching, these moral lessons given by men that spoke its simple language, and put themselves on a level with it? The Rabbis themselves, whose erudition raised the great monument of the Halacha, did not disdain to speak to the populace and, dropping all scientific apparel, array themselves in the simplicity of heart and the ingenuousness of the humble men they addressed. A number of names might be cited.

One will suffice, that of Akiba, the first redactor of the Mishna, whom the admiration of his contemporaries placed by the side of Moses, and who, says the Talmud, was great in the Halacha and equally great in the Haggada. Nevertheless, it is easy to recognize two well-marked tendencies, two distinct movements, and at first sight it is evident that, though these two movements were sometimes parallel, they might sometimes contradict each other. Were all the Halachist doctors Aggadists Obviously not. The Halacha and the Haggada demanded opposite gifts; they illustrate the natural opposition between science and poetry. Again, the Haggada was calculated to bring about by insensible degrees the predominance of inner religion over external forms and the depreciation of observances and ceremonies- an instinctive tendency bound to work its effect upon logical minds; a germ of dissidence apt to grow and lead to the separation of Halachists and Aggadists.

These inferences find full confirmation in the study of facts. We are fortunate to be able to shelter ourselves behind the authority of the learned author of the Essay on the History of Palestine; "The inhabitants of Galilee," says M. Derenbourg (p.

350), "in ill repute on account of their ignorance of legal affairs, seem to have replaced subtlety of mind by ardor of heart, and supplied lack of ability for brilliant tilts in scholastic discussions by excessive energy of feeling and tricks of expression, original rather than delicate. One always ends by attaching little value to what one is ignorant of, and has not been able to learn, especially if success comes in despite of ignorance, and seems to come precisely from a quarter despised by the informed and instructed. The merchant Hanania, who converted the young prince of Adiabene to Judaism, did not scruple to absolve him from the duty of circumcision, considering it binding only on the seed of Abraham. The Aggadists, indeed, learned from Isaiah and even Jeremiah a certain disdain for ceremonial observances, which naturally reacted on the Halachists occupied with hairsplitting casuistry on the subject of those very ceremonies... Doubtless there were men who, though devoted to Rabbinic science, still occupied themselves with the instruction of the people at the synagogues in religious truths, which they sought to support with texts from the poetic portions of the Scriptures. But it is equally certain that others, by reason of temperament or inclination, gave themselves up to the one or the other development of Judaism exclusively. A glance at the Talmuds and the Midrashim suffices to reveal many names that figure in the Halacha, and are never met with in the Agada, as likewise Aggadists are found that are never mentioned in the Halachic discussions. To become an Aggadist only ardent conviction, lively imagination, and facility of invention were necessary- qualities not rare in times when oppression by aliens revives national zeal, and among a people that receives impressions rapidly, and promptly translates them into words. An Aggadist, then, could be produced without great difficulty, but long and serious study was necessary to penetrate to the depths of the Halacha. As the value of a thing is usually measured by the difficulties surmounted in its acquisition, the Halachists in their turn underrated the preachers or Aggadists, who, as said above, were not always charmed with the

# THE TALMUD

deductions of the Rabbis.

The Talmuds have preserved numerous indications of the slight repute in which the Aggadists were held by the Rabbis. If, however, the passages relating to this subject contradict each other, and if a Rabbi who but now extolled preaching speaks of it scornfully, we must not be surprised; they are judgments rendered under the influence of an Agada recently heard, and are determined by the more or less respectful attitude assumed in it towards Rabbinic studies. Disdain for the Halacha has found a place particularly in Christian writings and in the school of St. Paul. We think that we do not err in maintaining that at its birth the AgGadists were the most powerful auxiliaries of Christianity."

The results of historic criticism, then, establish the justness of the deductions reached by psychological observation. Human nature is too feeble to attain to a complete expansion of all its faculties; one of them at least is sacrificed to the cultivation of the others. Some pursue the ideal of the good, others that of the true, and only in rare instances is the perfection at once of knowledge and of goodness reached. Surely what is true of the individual is with greater force true of the crowd, in which tendencies realize and assert themselves more powerfully. Judaism is proof thereof, but not the only proof. Without going far afield, we find an illustration of a similar phenomenon in the Catholicism of the middle ages. It likewise offers the spectacle of these two opposite currents swaying the minds of men in the rivalry of its two monastic orders, the Benedictine and the Franciscan, the learned order and the mendicant order, which epitomize their duties, the one, in the pursuit of the true, the other, in the pursuit of the good, and which- to conclude with an expression of the Rabbis- might have said, the former, truth saves from death, the latter, charity saves from death. It may be useful to give here a list of the books composing

# THE TALMUD

the Haggada literature. This literature comprises only exegetic explanations or Scripture interpretations given in the synagogues or in popular homilies. The epithet Midrash, or explanation, was applied to them. The chief collections of Midrashim are the following: The great Pesikta, or Pesikta Rabbathi, of Palestinian origin, attributed to R. Cahana. The Midrash Rabba, Haggadistic commentary on the Pentateuch and the books of Esther, Ecclesiastes, Song of Songs, Ruth, and Lamentations. The Midrash Yelamdenu and the Tanchuma on the Pentateuch. The Midrash Shokher Tob on the Psalms and the Proverbs. The compilation of these Midrashim, most of them very ancient, cannot be traced back further than the sixth century.

A number of Midrashim on the Prophets have been lost, or are still reposing on the shelves of various European libraries. In the twelfth century, a Rabbi, Simeon, conceived the idea of making a compilation of diverse Midrashim. This compilation, which bears the name Yalkut Shimeoni, or Simeon's Collection, has preserved a number of Midrashim that would otherwise not have reached us.

# THE TALMUD

## PART SECOND

## THE FORMATION OF THE TALMUD - THE SPIRIT OF ITS FORMATION

The essential character of every revealed religion is immutability. Claiming the exclusive possession of the truth, it cannot admit that it modifies itself at the will of the times, and follows the march of human thought in its successive transformations. For truth issuing from God is immutable; an expression of divinity, it may apply to itself the biblical word, "I am that I am." Like Catholicism, Judaism declares emphatically that religion has suffered no change during the long series of centuries. As it was revealed to Moses, as such it has perpetuated itself to our day, unaffected by the influence of the ages and of diverse civilizations. Potentially it was contained in the principles taught at Sinai, and Moses, seeing the future of the nation and the religion founded by himself unroll before him, could embrace in a single glance the vast, yet homogeneous succession of laws and doctrines. Now Judaism finds its expression in the Talmud, which is not a remote suggestion and a faint echo thereof, but in which it has become incarnate, in which it has taken form, passing from the state of an abstraction into the domain of real things. The study of Judaism is that of the Talmud, as the study of the Talmud is that of Judaism. To wish to understand one without entering upon the explanation of the other is chimerical. They are two inseparable things, or better, they are one and the same.

But the expression Talmud is here limited to Halacha. For, besides its information on various sciences, besides its moral principles which have been codified, and so fall under the Halacha, the Haggada contains only legends, fables, the whole poetic literature of the Midrashim. As one would not think of

# THE TALMUD

going to the legends of the Virgin, of the saints, and of Satan for the study of the Catholic dogmas, so the religious idea of Judaism in its primary and essential form must not be sought in Midrashic literature. To the Halacha alone, then, attention must be paid in order to understand the Talmud and trace the law of its genesis. It is the only letter in which Judaism has embodied itself. In point of fact, when the Synagogue is questioned about the origin of tradition, we are told that the oral Law ascends to the Sinaitic revelation, that its development is deductive, and shaped by unalterable principles, and that this astounding efflorescence of Halachoth is only the natural expansion of a primitive law and idea. "The Scriptures, the decisions of the Rabbis, and all that a reverent disciple of the Law may teach, were given to Moses on Sinai."

## I: THE HALACHA ACCORDING TO THE SYNAGOGUE

It is a cardinal principle of Judaism that, along with the code comprised in the Pentateuch, Moses received from God on Mount Sinai an oral Law, which is the commentary developed from the written Law. Not a precept, not a decision, not a ceremonial injunction was left unaccompanied by oral explanations, which Moses was to transmit by word of mouth. These explanations, moreover, were of the same sacred character as the written Law. In its conciseness, the latter often is obscure; it is incomplete, for usually it proceeds by examples; sometimes even it consists of apparent contradictions, sometimes of seemingly useless repetitions. Examples abound: "At the mouth of two witnesses, or at the mouth of three witnesses shall the matter be established," it says in Deuteronomy XIX, 15. Is it two? Is it three? In Leviticus XXI, 12, the high priest is forbidden to go out of the sanctuary. Under what circumstances? Is he to be shut up in it all his life? Elsewhere it is said: "Thou shalt kill animals as I have commanded thee." Where is this command? A second passage relative to this ordinance would be sought in vain in the whole Pentateuch. The obligation to "lay Tephilin," one of the essential observances of Judaism, is barely indicated by a word. On the other hand, the following is found in three different places: "Thou shalt not seethe a kid in its mother's milk." Elsewhere historic facts in complete contradiction to the Law are told, although the men to whom they are attributed are charged with the duty of teaching the Law.

The pious king Hezekiah celebrates the Passover in the second month, although Moses fixes it on the fifteenth day of the first month. The prophet Elijah offers a sacrifice on Carmel, in spite of the law in Deuteronomy forbidding sacrifices outside of the Temple. Finally, in another sphere of ideas, a striking feature of the Books of Moses is their unbroken silence concerning primary dogmas of the Jewish religion, the dogmas of the immortality of the soul and the future life. These are not the only examples. A considerable number of similar facts, of obscure laws that cannot do without explanation, of important omissions, and of apparent contradictions, might be collated. It is evident, then, that the written Law stands in need of a perpetual commentary.

This is the commentary received by Moses on Mount Sinai. Thence its name: The Law of Moses from Sinai (Halacha le-Moshi mis-Sinai = lex ad Mosem e Sinai). This Law descended orally from generation to generation. "Moses," says the Mishna, "received the (traditional) Law on Sinai, and transmitted it to Joshua; Joshua transmitted it to the Elders; the Elders transmitted it to the Prophets, and the Prophets to the Men of the Great Assembly."

The Great Assembly, to which the last three prophets, Haggai, Zechariah, and Malachi, belonged, finally transmit the oral Law to the teachers that succeed each other from the coming of the Seleucidae into Syria to the second century of the

# THE TALMUD

Christian era. The oral Law was never to be entrusted to writing, but was to remain in the memory of men and form a living tradition. But when the misfortunes that began to break in upon the people in the days of the last Maccabees imperiled the preservation of the sacred pledge; when Titus had destroyed the Temple, and Hadrian had scattered the Jewish people, and proscribed the study of the Law, it was feared that the chain of tradition might be ruptured, and the oral Law disappear in the cataclysm that swept away Jewish nationality. For the sake of the welfare of Judaism, R. Judah the Holy decided to violate the prohibition and reduce the oral Law to writing. This was the origin of the Mishna.

The synagogue declares that from the Sinaitic revelation until the rebuilding of the Temple, after the return from the Captivity, even until within a short time before the Christian era, the oral Law maintained itself intact, without uncertainty or obscurity. After the return, the novel conditions surrounding the nation brought up new problems for which tradition offered no solution. What were the Rabbis to do? Obviously classify them by means of certain ratiocinative processes under cases provided for by tradition. These exegetic processes themselves are taught by tradition. God had foreseen that a day would come when certain religious prescriptions would sink into oblivion, when new questions would obtrude themselves, and He gave unto Moses a hermeneutic system, by virtue of which the decisions of the oral Law might be rediscovered in the written Law, all the teachings of tradition might be brought into connection with the text, and general principles confidently applied to new details and unforeseen cases. The only thing to be done, therefore, was to make the points under discussion submit to these hermeneutic processes. But differences of opinion might thus arise. For, though the applicability of certain principles might be so obvious as to force immediate and unanimous assent, sometimes there might, on the other hand, be reason for hesitation and discussion.

# THE TALMUD

In these cases a vote was decisive, likewise in accordance with a principle established by the Scriptures, that, to employ the biblical expression, the multitude ought to be followed. A majority makes the law. The following account from the Mishna is a curious illustration. "Akabia ben Mahalalel maintained four propositions. The Rabbis said to him: Abandon them, and we shall give you the title of the chief of the Great Council. He replied; I prefer to be considered a fool all the days of my life to appearing infamous for a single instant before God by surrendering my convictions in exchange for honors... Nevertheless, at the point of death, he said to his son; Abandon the four propositions that I have taught thee- And why didst thou not yield? Because I had received them from teachers as numerous as those who had taught my adversaries the opposite opinions, and I supported what I had learned as firmly as they maintained their traditions. But as for you, you have learned the four decisions only from me, and an individual's opinions ought to give way before those of a number- To this principle add the other that numbers being equal, the opinions of the older teachers prevail over those of the more recent ones. And that is just. For truth is subject to change as the distance from its origin across the ages lengthens; and though divergence of opinions began to manifest itself only very late, and Hillel and Shammai, at the beginning of the Christian era, were at variance on only three points, yet in the space of three centuries differences multiplied so extensively as to produce the vast 'sea of the Talmud.' It is natural, then, that an opinion which has come down to us through few intermediaries should have more weight than one that has passed through many mouths. An Amora, or teacher of the Law posterior to the compilation of the Mishna, cannot prevail against a Tana, or teacher of the Mishna, no more than a Tana can enforce an opinion opposed by the Dibri Sopherim, the words of the Scribes.

With these principles regulating the discussion, the

# THE TALMUD

development was most simple; nothing was left to arbitrary chance. Discussion reduced itself to a deductive process. New laws were sacred by the same warrant as the revealed laws, since the latter enjoined the former by implication. The work of the Rabbis consisted simply in educing them, and we arrive at the explanation of the Talmudic sentence: "The Scriptures, Tradition, the decisions of the Rabbis, and all that a reverent disciple of the Law may teach, were given to Moses on Sinai."

Such is this theory of tradition, a theory remarkable for simplicity and consistency, and based upon a profoundly true view. Even if criticism cannot throw brilliant light upon the history of tradition in its primitive stages, it cannot fail to confirm the correctness of the view, that the development of the Halacha was logical and necessary, as we propose to demonstrate in the following pages.

# THE TALMUD

## II: HISTORY OF THE FORMATION OF THE HALACHA

One of the most curious problems in the history of religions assuredly is that presented by the state of the Jews on their return from the Captivity. Up to the last moments of the monarchy, the minds of the people are controlled by one of two religious currents. On the one side is popular superstition, the grossly sensual idolatry borrowed from Phoenicia, against which the Jeremiahs and the Ezekiels thundered, often in vain. On the other side is the elevated, austere spirituality of the Prophets, who seek to lead back the multitude to the feet of Jehovah's altars, and energetically struggle against the depraving tendencies of paganism. On the return from the Exile, two changes have taken place. The whole people has rallied about the religious chiefs, and the latter are no longer Prophets, but Scribes. Thenceforth the streets of Jerusalem do not resound with the eloquent invectives of the Nebiim. Instead, the explanations and the commentaries of the Sopherim fill the schools and the synagogues. We no longer have dealings with an inconstant people hesitating between Baal and Jehovah, but with a nation that has made its choice, and enthusiastically accepts and develops a cult, that is, a well coordinated system of beliefs, laws, and practices. Its literature suits itself to this transformation. No longer the rich and vigorous efflorescence to which we owe such masterpieces as the Psalms, Isaiah, Job, it has become severe, dogmatic, scholastic instruction, which after eight laborious centuries will result in the Talmud. In a word, Hebraism is at an end, Judaism is born.

What are the causes of the transformation? What series of circumstances could have effected it in so limited a period as the Captivity? Dark questions, the answers to which may be guessed at, but the elements of an unimpeachable solution are lacking. This is not the place to examine and discuss the

## THE TALMUD

problem; the statement of the change must suffice.

A new era begins for Israel. The whole nation crowds about the Sopherim to hear the explanation of the Law. It is learned by heart, it is commented upon. Schools of Rabbis spring up, which charge themselves with the duty of teaching and explaining the sacred word. The Bible, the Book, especially the Pentateuch, Mikra, that is, Reading; this is the only mental nourishment indulged in by the people. It is the aim of all science, and it is science itself. For all things flow from the Bible, as all converge towards it. The admonition addressed to Joshua, "Thou shalt meditate therein day and night," has become a reality. In a word, it is the axis on which turns the whole activity of the Jewish mind. Thus originates and grows the study of the Law, which is called to play so considerable a role, and whence springs the body of traditional laws that will constitute the Talmud.

How do these traditional laws originate? Unless we accept the theory of their Sinaitic origin, affirmed, but not demonstrated, by the Synagogue, the historic documents fail to make direct answer to this question. The first traces of these traditions are met with late, in the Septuagint, in the Books of the Maccabees, in the Book of Daniel, contemporary with the Maccabees; but they suffice to put it beyond a doubt that as early as the time of Antiochus Epiphanes a number of decisions were definitely established; that even then the ceremonies connected with the cult and not indicated in the Pentateuch were regulated, in a word, that a rather extensive system of observances and laws existed. Doubtless it was during the long period of more than 250 years from Ezra to the Maccabean rebellion that this system grew up, and imposed itself upon the Jewish nation. Josephus passes over this religious development with profound silence; but it is well known that for this historian, more or less scrupulous concerning facts, the history of beliefs, ideas, and

# THE TALMUD

religious institutions was almost as though non-existent.

However, it is beyond question that the Men of the Great Synagogue developed the Mosaic prescriptions, and especially by their personal authority raised 'a hedge' about the Law. It is not possible to trace the traditional system further back with any degree of certainty. The critical study of several Mishnic traditions beginning with Hasmonean times enables us to follow the development of Jewish legislation, at once religious and civil. The searching investigation of juridic points led to its gradual extension. In the civil law the extension presents no peculiar features, its only object being the protection of the interests of the individual and the promotion of the intercourse and the transactions of the citizens with each other. But with the religious law the case was different. Eminently restrictive in character, it was developed to the point of burdening daily life with numerous observances. Its decisions multiplied indefinitely, and each became the fountainhead for others. Some, laid down as principles, were to bring forth, when fecundated by ratiocination, a close-linked chain of endless prescriptions embracing every moment of human life. To be clear, let us take examples.

A Pentateuch verse says: "Thou shalt not seethe a kid in its mother's milk." An old tradition, first expressed in the Septuagint, explains this verse by the prohibition to cook meat with milk food. This prohibition, universally recognized, the Rabbis take as their point of departure. They deduce therefrom a group of special laws, which, in turn, will prove no less fruitful. For instance, it will give rise to the prohibition of eating meat with milk food, of eating milk food immediately after meat, of using the same vessel for meat and milk, and many others. And the logical deductions will go on to the bitter end, nor shrink from the consideration of the minutest details connected with the kitchen- In the Pentateuch we read: "Thou shalt not eat flesh that is torn of beasts in the field." From this prohibition an entire code will be developed. In fact, what matters it whether it was torn in the city or in the field, so long as it is the carrion of an animal killed by a wild beast or dead of a disease? The purpose evidently is to forbid eating the flesh of a sick or unhealthy animal. But when is an animal sick or unhealthy? Thence so and so many new laws to determine all the cases falling under the interdiction. Again, the prohibition of working on the Sabbath. What is meant by the word work? Some more new laws to demonstrate what is forbidden and up to what limits- Nor is this all. To these laws, logically and unavoidably deduced from more general, long recognized laws, must be added ordinances of recent institution.

One Rabbi maintains somewhere in the Talmud that certain ones of these ordinances were later considered traditional, Sinaitic laws. Besides, there are measures and decrees (Tekanoth, Gezeroth) passed by the Sanhedrin at the dictate and under the stress of circumstances, which, from the moment of their promulgation, had the authority of religious laws. Thus is woven an intricate web of prescriptions, ceaselessly reproducing others of their kind, which, enthusiastically accepted by a people enamored of its religious system, are at once consecrated by usage. Such is the work to which the schools devote themselves, especially in the century preceding and in that following the destruction of the second Temple. By that time the multiplicity of laws was so great that the links connecting a particular law with the primitive law, biblical or traditional, from which it was derived, could be grasped only with difficulty. Recourse was therefore had to artificial methods for the purpose of establishing a direct connection between the Pentateuch text on the one hand, and the early traditional laws, the deduced laws of whatsoever derivation, and the laws of recent institution, on the other. There were first Hillel's seven rules of interpretation, from which R.

# THE TALMUD

Ishmael evolved thirteen. Then came the curious, bold method that Akiba has the distinction of having applied and developed with undaunted consistency. It is based on the principle that in the Scriptures nothing is superfluous, neither phrase, nor word, nor particle, nor letter; that down to the most insignificant detail everything has peculiar value, and that besides the obvious meaning of the text the intelligent mind ought to discover a thousand hidden meanings, a thousand occult hints. Such and such a word, contrary to usage, is written with a waw; in another the waw is lacking apparently without reason; here the word and is redundant, there the conjunction is suppressed- all indications of half-revealed things, of laws, if the verse has a legal bearing, of facts, if the verse is of another character. The book of Genesis, for example, opens with the words: "In the beginning God created heaven and earth." The word 'heaven' in Hebrew is preceded by the particle eth, usually the sign of the accusative, but sometimes also meaning with. That particle must have some meaning, says Akiba, and he explains the verse in the following manner: "God created with (the celestial hosts, that is, the stars) heaven and earth." This method, which in principle was recognized by the Fathers of the Church, St. Basil, St. Jerome, St. Chrysostom, was applied to all the religious prescriptions established by the Rabbis. Thenceforth the ordinances of the Rabbis and the practices sanctified by time, but lacking a sure foundation, were clothed with a sacred character, and animated with new life, by contact with the Holy Scriptures. The importance of the method is patent. In modern society the law preserves its character for majesty in the eyes of the people. Yet it is considered a human work, subject to error, capable of modification or amelioration according to changing needs. It is respected, because it has been freely assented to by all, and the people honor in it the wish and work of all. In a society pre-eminently religious, like that of the Jews, the same feeling cannot prevail. A number of Rabbinic prescriptions could doubtless have been shown to originate in ancient and venerable

## THE TALMUD

traditions, but many were of recent institution.

How could they be urged upon the people and made to influence their manners, if they were not clothed with a sacred character, and in whatsoever way possible justified by the very letter of the Scriptures? This method, likewise, by providing the shelter of the Law, opened the way to the modifications and the useful reforms made necessary by circumstances. Thus Judaism accommodated itself to the constantly shifting needs of a society constantly in a state of upheaval, and, consecrating the aspirations of each new generation, it could develop and progress boldly on the path of reforms. This method secured the religion against the inert worship of the word and the letter, snatched it away from stagnation, and, by the flux and movement it produced, vivified and fortified faith. Thus it sanctioned at once tradition, which thenceforth was fixed, and future innovations that might crop up.

Did the people understand immediately the immense import of the procedure? We do not know, but certainly they conceived profound admiration for the man able to educe "bushels of decisions from every stroke of a letter." Arbitrary as the method may seem to us, the favor it met with may be explained by the ardent desire of the people, pointed out above, to find everything in the Holy Scriptures. They are looked upon by the people as the source of all knowledge. The Rabbis invent nothing; they merely rediscover in the Sacred Writings the laws that they establish. Far from setting out on the search for the unknown, they repeat tradition. They are the Tanaim, 'the repeaters,' and the work taught by them in the schools is the Mishna, that is, 'the repetition.' The aspirations of the crowd, then, are satisfied by this method, which, moreover, appeals to its admirers by its boldness and ingenuity; hence its triumph. However, the work of the teachers was not approved by the entire nation. One class of society was outspoken in its

# THE TALMUD

opposition to the doctrines and the instruction of the Pharisees.

The aristocracy, the rich priestly families, saw with displeasure the growth of an inconvenient legislative system, which compelled them to a life of austerities and sacrifices far from charming to their taste. The party of the Sadducees can be traced back to the establishment of the sacerdotal royalty of the Hasmoneans, to the day on which an aristocracy began to form about the reigning family. The Sadducees admitted all the religious traditions that time had consecrated up to their day. But they were opposed to the development of traditional legislation, and as Akiba's method was its most powerful instrument, they combated it with all their ability. Though living up to traditions that could not be explained by the Pentateuch, they insisted that they abided only by the pure and simple meaning of the text; they followed, or at least pretended to follow, scrupulously the letter of the Law, and observed its explicit injunctions, refusing to modify them by the ordinances of recent institution. They had no schools whose disciples might have been recruited from among the people. But the priests formed a college, and among themselves they propagated their traditions, which, however, were rejected by the people. During the great upheaval that terminated in the catastrophe of the year 70, the Sadducees, who were sincere Jews, and repudiated only the exaggerations of the Pharisaic system, fused with the people, and all dissension was forgotten in the face of the common danger.

But after the destruction of the Temple, when the Rabbis established their schools at Jabne, in the north of Palestine, the priests, whose services had become superfluous, exiled themselves to the Daroma, or the South, and there established rival schools, in which they taught the sacerdotal tradition. While Akiba's numerous disciples developed the word of the master, R. Ishmael ben Elisha, high priest, taught in the Dar6ma. Rigorously confining to its narrowest limits the system of

## THE TALMUD

interpretation adopted by Akiba, he explained the Pentateuch according to its simplest sense. He thrust out of the Books of Moses the lessons that the school of the north made dominant, and preserved the variants that ancient priestly tradition had sanctified. We owe to him commentaries on all the Books of the Pentateuch except Genesis.

They are the Mechilta (measure), commentary on Exodus; Sifra (book), commentary on Leviticus, also called Torath Cohanim, or Law of the Priests, on account of the numerous Levitical prescriptions which form the object of the third Book of Moses; finally, Sifre (books), the commentaries on Numbers and Deuteronomy. These are the only works bequeathed by the school of Daroma. The school, in fact, soon vanished into darkness, being each day more and more obscured by the brilliant light irradiating from its northern rival. The mentioned works, moreover, were preserved only because the Pharisaic schools adopted them after having modified them by touches changing their character.

However, the alterations were not so radical but that under the Pharisaic layer traces remained of the Sadducean, or at least sacerdotal, method. Thanks to these vestiges, the historic science of our day has succeeded in rediscovering the spirit of the original work by a circumstantial study of the language, of the Halachoth, and the Pentateuch injunctions involved in them. By re-establishing the text three-fourths effaced, a species of palimpsest, it not only restored the work of Ishmael ben Elisha's school, but demonstrated the permanence of Sadducean instruction.

Akiba, however, had not yet finished his work. To have connected all the traditional and recently instituted laws with the Pentateuch was not sufficient. It was necessary to coordinate and unite them into a sort of code. In fact, in the schools the

# THE TALMUD

commentaries and the instruction of the Rabbis had at first followed the text of the Law, and the order of its chapters and verses determined the order of the Halachoth. But when the Halachoth, by the successive labors of the schools, had multiplied extensively, it became impossible to teach them in that order. Each verse was accompanied by a commentary of infinite length; the text disappeared, buried under the notes. A classification thus became necessary, and this again was Akiba's work. His master mind succeeded in putting order into the vast chaos of decisions. But he could do no more than trace the outlines. The Roman hangman prevented him from finishing the work, which his school continued, and a disciple of his followers, R. Judah the Holy, of the illustrious family of Hillel, had the glory of making the final compilation of the Mishna and attaching his name thereto.

It was an important achievement, this codification of the oral law, and one big with results. Once taught from the written word in the Mishna, Tradition received its final consecration. It ceased to be tradition to become a new Law- a Law completer, preciser, and clearer than the ancient Law, which found itself relegated to the background. "It is better to be occupied with the Mishna, than with the Law," said the Rabbis; "the Law may be compared to water, but the Mishna is wine." Why, in fact, should one lose time in puzzling over the original text, when complete explanation is within reach of all, when the Mishna contains both text and commentary? So tradition, from being a commentary on the Law, itself becomes a second law, a Deuterosis, to use the expression of the Fathers of the Church, and takes the place of the first. Thereafter, the work of the schools, thought to be at an end, will be resumed. The long labor expended on the Pentateuch and terminating in the Mishna will be applied to the Mishna to produce finally the Gemara. The text of the Mishna will be taken up again and discussed.

# THE TALMUD

Every Rabbinic opinion, whether anonymous, that is, admitted by all, or cited with its author's name, that is, with every possible reservation, will be argued, debated, developed, explained. Obscure points will be illuminated, and so again new decisions will be arrived at. And after three centuries of discussion, the Gemara will be finished, and the Talmud closed. Thus a new era begins with the compilation of the Mishna. But a new era must have a new name. The doctors of the Mishna had been Tanaim, repeaters; the teachers of the epoch upon which we are about to enter are called Amoraim, discoursers- two well chosen names, in each case characterizing exactly the nature of the instruction. For if, on the one hand, the Tanaim only taught tradition, only reproduced and repeated decisions received from ancient times to transmit them to disciples, then, on the other hand, this tradition once fixed, there remained nothing more than to discuss the Law and to discourse.

This work of the teachers of the Gemara does not withdraw itself wholly from foreign influences. While they are building up the code on the solid basis of the Mishna, a neighboring nation, whose formidable power they know only too well, is engaged about a similar task, and with incomparable force and marvellous genius raises the monumental *Corpus Juris civilis*, on which will be propped the legal systems of Europe. How was it possible for the Rabbis to escape the influence that Roman legislation, whose rigor and formalism they should have been the first to admire, could exercise upon them? In point of fact, the civil law of the Talmud is impregnated in almost all its parts with the spirit of the Roman system. Even formulas and expressions borrowed from Rome can be found in it. Certain departments of legislation, such as the laws on slavery and prescription, for which the Pentateuch furnishes not a hint, or sketches barely the shadow of a theory, are almost entirely inspired by Roman legislation. But, all they borrow takes on modifications under the manipulation of the Rabbis. The Jewish mind transformed the alien elements by impressing upon them its peculiar character. And from this vast crucible, in which three centuries had melted down the materials of diverse origin gathered by the schools, was to emerge the essentially uniform and homogeneous work of Talmudic legislation.

# THE TALMUD

## III: INFLUENCE OF EVENTS ON THE DEVELOPMENT OF THE HALACHA

In the preceding pages, we studied only the internal development of the Halacha. It is now time to consider whether external circumstances exercised influence upon this development; whether and up to what point they trammeled or favored it. Although its first traces are found only in the Maccabean epoch, it is well known that the work of the Jewish schools resulting in the Talmud began on the return from the Captivity. From that period until the time of the final redaction of the Talmud, four great events mark the history of Judea; the persecutions of Antiochus Epiphanes, followed by the re-establishment of the kingdom by the Hasmoneans; the birth of Christianity; the destruction of the Temple, and the last revolt of the Jews under Hadrian. We shall examine the influence upon the formation of the Halacha attributable to each of these events. In the long and tranquil years of the Persian domination, Judaism, under the direction of the Men of the Great Synagogue, could grow unshackled, and instruction, little by little penetrating the mass of the people, formed the national mind. The persecutions of Antiochus, therefore, were nothing more than a passing storm, which, we may well believe, effected a revival and strengthening of religious feeling. We say, we may well believe, for we possess no documents to acquaint us with the precise nature of their influence. The triumph of the Maccabees again insured a certain tranquility for the Jews, thanks to which the Rabbis, as under the Persian domination, could calmly prosecute their long continuing work. But Rome enters upon the scene. Pompey takes possession of Jerusalem, and desecrates the Sanctuary. Soon Judea falls under the iron yoke of the procurators, whose odious tyranny leads to the terrible insurrection of the year 65. The history of the heroic, superhuman struggle ending with the burning of the Temple and the annihilation of the Jewish state, is well known. It

## THE TALMUD

would seem that a revolution like this ought to react powerfully upon religious conditions. The results, however, do not correspond to the greatness of the catastrophe; for the influence was material rather than moral.

With the destruction of the Temple disappeared a part of the cult and a whole set of ceremonies. All connected with the sacrifices was abrogated by the force of circumstances. But the rest of the cult remained intact, no cause, moreover, presenting itself to modify its spirit. The fact is that, though the Jewish nationality was crushed, the religion was not persecuted. The political mold shattered, the religious mold remained perfect, and preserved the hope of the re-establishment of national independence. This is what Vespasian did not understand, and in permitting R. Jochanan ben Zakkar to transport his school to Jabne, he did not realize that he was allowing a fire to be kindled on a new hearth of insurrection. Sixty years after the fall of Jerusalem, in fact, the grandsons of those who saw the ruin of the 'Holy House,' rise at the call of Akiba, rush to arms, chase the Romans out of Palestine, reconquer their land, summon all their brethren of the Empire, and for an instant re-erect the kingdom of their ancestors. It is a grave moment, for this struggle is to decide, not only upon Israel's fate, but also upon that of the new sect that Israel has permitted to go forth from his midst. The Christianity of about the year 70 had not acquired sufficient power to feel the consequences of the catastrophe. A little sect without influence, it found protection in its own feebleness.

But from that time until Hadrian, it grew and extended itself, and the germs of dissidence present from its birth in the antagonism of Peter and Paul developed. The Church was divided into two chief sects: the Judeo-Christians, disciples of Peter, and the adepts of Paul. The Judeo-Christians still count themselves as Jews, and accept all the religious teachings of the Rabbis, adding only the article of faith that the Messiah had

## THE TALMUD

come in the person of Jesus. Paul and his disciples reject all the ceremonies, all the traditional laws, more than that, even the Law of Moses, and profess a new doctrine, whence Catholicism was later to issue. This is the situation when Bar Coziba, the Son of the Star, the new Messiah whom Akiba salutes, stirs up the Jews in revolt against Tinnius Rufus. The Judeo-Christians, mindful of the Master's word, "My kingdom is not of this world," refuse to fight at the side of the Jews. Coziba, by threats of punishment, forces them to take up arms. But when Severus triumphs, and Bethar falls into the power of the Romans, the most terrible vengeance strikes all who bear the name Jew.

Hadrian does not fall into Vespasian's error; he perceives that the Jews are to be feared so long as anything recalls the memory of their nationality, and religious ceremonials are proscribed on pain of death. "Why art thou condemned to death?" says a Talmudic text. "Because I observed the law of circumcision"- "Why art thou led away to punishment"- "Because I was faithful to the Sabbath."- "Why art thou scourged?"- "Because I obeyed the injunction of the Lord." In the face of these consequences, the Judeo-Christians break the last bond uniting them with the Jews, and throw themselves into the arms of the Paulinians. The Church, which preaches the abolition of ceremonies, sees her triumph assured.

But if the result of this war is to precipitate the Church along the road upon which she has just entered so resolutely, it ought to have the opposite influence on Judaism, plunging it deeper into Pharisaism. And that for two reasons. The first, producing an effect only during a limited period, is the religious persecution which Hadrian himself enforces against the Jews. For, the more the ceremonies are persecuted, and the more the people feels its lot bound up with them, the greater grows their importance in the eyes of the believer, the more do they tend to become absolute. Then, when the persecutions abated, and the

# THE TALMUD

people began to breathe more freely, it was necessary to institute a separation from the Church, which gained territory day after day. The differences dividing the two religions had to be marked more clearly. And the more unreservedly growing Christianity opened its ample bosom to the pagan nations, the more Judaism inclined to retreat, jealously withdrawing into itself and multiplying its practices and observances from day to day, from hour to hour. The abyss parting it from the Christians and the pagans deepened. It remained isolated in the midst of hostile nations, and this isolation constituted its strength. Thus became possible the strange phenomenon, unique in history, I believe, of a people dispersed to the four corners of the earth, yet one, of a nation without a land, yet living. The miracle was accomplished by a book, the Talmud. The Talmud was the ensign which served as a rallying point for the dispersed of Israel.

The thousand austere and minute practices that it enjoins were so many strong bonds attaching one to the other. Thus, by a curious series of actions and reactions, the religious movement that gave birth to the Mishna brought about the national uprising under Hadrian. Through its influence on Christianity, this rebellion reacted indirectly on the religious movement that produced the Talmud. And the Talmud, in turn, maintained the unity of the people, conquered and crushed, yet none the less living and resisting.

# THE TALMUD

## IV: SPIRIT OF THE HALACHIC DEVELOPMENT

Let us now cast a glance backwards, and take a bird's-eye view of this effective development of Pharisaic formalism. We are at once struck by its system of observances having relation to every moment of life. The believer finds himself enmeshed in a net-work of prescriptions, which close in upon him on all sides, and reduce him to never ending slavery- slavery accepted freely and with joy, for this sacred, a thousand times blessed yoke is the condition of happiness. Chained down by the many links that his religion has forged into a system around him, he has only to follow without fatigue or effort the divine commandments. He has no need for long reflection upon his duties and for much reasoning on the rules of conduct, absolved as he is by religion, which has done all this work for him. Each day, each hour, is unalterably arranged by regulations from on high. In the morning, prayers and thanksgivings; at noon, prayers and thanksgivings; in the evening, prayers and thanksgivings; benedictions before the meal, after the meal, benedictions. At sight of the imposing phenomena of nature, of a storm, the sea, the first spring blossoms, thanksgivings. Thanksgivings for a new enjoyment, for unexpected good fortune, on eating new fruits, at the announcement of a happy event. Prayers of resignation at the news of a misfortune. At the tomb of a beloved being, set prayers; words all prepared to console the sorrow stricken, who have just been overtaken by affliction. Every emotion and every feeling, the most fugitive as well as the most profound, are foreseen, noted, and embodied in a formula of prayer or of benediction. In the most solemn moments of life as in the most vulgar, when the soul forgets itself and allows itself to drop into the prose of daily routine, or when, crushed under the load of lively emotions, it gives way, yielding to its powerlessness, the believer finds himself in the presence of a commandment, of a Mitzwa to be accomplished,

# THE TALMUD

recalling him to heavenly things, sanctifying the present hour, and keeping him in perpetual communication with the divine. If he wishes to breathe forth his feelings and give them definite shape, he finds ready-made formulas at hand, which he has but to repeat with fervor in order to pour out his soul before God. The Israelite then, has no need of painful efforts in seeking the road to salvation. It is wide open to him, thanks to his religion, that tender, provident mother who convoys him to happiness, provided he obeys the divine prescriptions, and with docility goes whither God leads him. Such is the system the rearing of which the Talmud has pursued with the force of bold logic. Curiously enough, nowhere can the precisely formulated expression of this system be found. Moreover, it is well known that the Synagogue has never summoned a Council to decree a dogma and impose it upon the faith of the nation. But whether a precise formula embodying their system was present in the minds of the Rabbis, or whether they unconsciously followed it out, it may none the less be abstracted in all its clearness from the very spirit of Halachic development; namely, impotence of human reason to direct itself in the search for truth, and the duty imposed upon religion to teach it truth.

In fact, is not this the system of all religions? Do they not one and all recognize the powerlessness of human reason to arrive at truth without assistance from above? Are they not all sent down from heaven to lead man to salvation? Judaism, then, has followed out a natural evolution, and perhaps this is the point of view to be assumed in explaining its derivation from Hebraism. Every religion is at first based upon ideal principles, principles of justice and charity, which for some time, in a vague and indeterminate form, satisfy certain ardent, religious spirits. But it cannot long persist in this indeterminate form; it clothes itself with a body, becomes a dogma, and is transformed from moral instruction, which it first was, into a positive religion. Then, if it is logical, it condemns itself to pursue the course

# THE TALMUD

boldly taken by Pharisaism. That is what we are taught by the theoretic conception of the religious idea, and that is what is proved by history. History tells us that every religion rests upon formalism. It tells us that Mohammedism, like Judaism, has arrived at a cult burdened with ceremonies. It shows us in Italic polytheism an infinite multiplicity of divinities directing the conduct of men. It shows us the Roman peasant trembling before the four thousand gods that presided over every act and moment of life and Lucretius delivering men from the chains of religion. It tells us that the Brahmin arrive at scholasticism comparable with the Talmud; that the doctrine of St. Paul itself, the doctrine founded on the rejection of every external observance, later gives birth to the *Summa Theologica* of St. Thomas Aquinas and to the system of ceremonies from which Protestantism was a reaction. It tells us, finally, that, if Protestantism alone has hitherto escaped this law, it is because it is a compromise between religion and philosophy, and that logic condemns it to end up either in formalism or in deism. Judaism, then, could not but pursue this course, and urged by the logic of things, which was favored by an array of circumstances destructive of the political existence of the nation, beneficent for its religious work, it pursued it to the end. Accordingly, the Talmud is the completest expression of a religious movement, and this code of endless prescriptions and minute ceremonials represents in its perfection the total work of the religious idea. In our eyes, this is its greatest title to the respect and the consideration of thinkers; this is its greatest merit. Certainly, Judaism may be regarded as austere and arid. It has not the splendor and brilliant exuberance of Greek or Hindu polytheism. We are far removed from the superabundant, vigorous poetry pervading the dazzling efflorescence of Aryan mythologies. Herein lies the great advantage of polytheism and pantheism over monotheism. But we are now not considering religions from the point of view of art; we are investigating only their dogmatic development, in so far as it can be abstracted and extricated from the rest of human

# THE TALMUD

faculties.

Taken in this way, that of Judaism has been most logical, since, without hesitation, it has proceeded to extreme consequences. If these consequences incur condemnation, then the system as a whole must be condemned, for the starting point is wrong. If the starting point is accepted, it is necessary to go to the bitter end, and endorse all the consequences. At all events, the Talmud has done so, and thanks to it we have in Judaism the completest, and consequently the most perfect, expression of the religious idea.

# THE TALMUD

## V: THE TALMUD IN THE MIDDLE AGES AND MODERN TIMES

### CONCLUSION

We have arrived at the end of our task. Endeavoring to apply the critical method to the investigation of the Talmud, we have demanded from an analytic study information on the elements composing it, and from an historic study the supreme law or idea governing its formation. Before we close this article, it may be proper to cast a glance at the fortunes of the book in the middle ages and in modern times and to indicate cursorily what science may still demand of it for the general history of humanity. When, a century after the compilation of the Palestinian Gemara, the Babylonian Talmud, in its turn, received its final shape, it was universally adopted in the Jewish schools, and the chiefs of the Academies, the Saboraim. (opinion givers, from the sixth to the eighth century), declaring the text fixed, decided that no more modifications could be introduced into it. Despite the persecutions of Jezdegerd II, Firuz, and Kobad, who closed the schools in Persia for a period of sixty-three years, and interrupted the teaching of the tradition, the Talmud became a classic to be studied and commented.

The Saboraim occupied themselves more especially with grammar, fixing the system of vowel points for the Bible, while the Geonim (excellencies, from the eighth to the ninth century), along with lexicographic work, devoted themselves especially to the study of the Talmud. Under their influence, this book formed the basis of instruction, and became for the schools what the Mishna had been for the Amoraim. To that epoch belongs the redaction of the Great Decisions (Halachoth Gedoloth), a work in which the principal decisions of the Talmud are classified in the order of the 613 commandments of the Pentateuch to which

# THE TALMUD

they had been attached, With the conquests of the Arabs, Jewish studies spread over Africa and Spain. A little later the movement takes possession of the Provence and of Italy, then of the regions to the north of the Loire as far as the German provinces on the Rhine. On all sides schools are opened, and remarkable works of various kinds published. R. Hananel undertakes an abridgment of the Halachic parts of the Talmud, which inspires, and in turn is displaced by, the similar work of R. Isaac of Fez (1013-1103). At the same time appears the complete Commentary by R. Solomon Isaaci, called Rashi, of Troyes in the Champagne, a masterpiece of brevity, precision, and clearness. In the following century, Maimonides, 'the eagle of the Synagogue,' publishes his Arabic commentary on the Mishna and the masterly work called Mishne Torah, 'the second law,' in which, embracing the whole domain of the Halacha, he seeks to systematize the vast mass of decisions. In France, Rashi created a school. With him directly is connected the galaxy of French Rabbis in the twelfth and thirteenth centuries, to whom the world owes the Talmudic glosses called Tosaphoth, or Additions.

It is this work of the Tosaphists together with Rashi's commentary, become a classic, that frames the text of the Mishna and the Gemara in all the editions. From France the movement spreads to north-western Germany, which in the thirteenth and the fourteenth century furnishes its contingent of commentaries and super-commentaries. These diverse works bear the same character. In all, the various decisions reached by the Gemara in the different cases discussed are compared; one is sought to be explained by the other, the import and extent of each are determined, and in all, the order or rather the disorder of the Gemara, somewhat palliated, is followed. With the exception of Maimonides, no one thought of introducing the light of method into this vast chaos and of classifying all the Halachoth logically. The German, Jacob ben Asher, in the fourteenth century, taking the Mishne Torah as his model, undertakes a methodical piece of

# THE TALMUD

work. For a century the attempt remains without imitation; the fifteenth century produces nothing for the Halacha. But in the sixteenth century appears the Polish school, whose works, though not characterized by the breadth of conception that distinguishes Maimonides' Mishne Torah, are remarkable for penetration and depth, perhaps lacking in that book. This school has for its aim the completion of R. Jacob ben Asher's work, and in 1567 Joseph Karo publishes his Shulhan Arukh (the prepared table), in which all the religious and civil laws of the Jews, article by article, are classified according to subjects. The codification of the Halacha is thereby completed, but not the work of the commentators, which continues upon the text of the Code during the eighteenth century, and in our day is not at an end in Bohemia, in Hungary, and in all the sections of the world where the Jews have most faithfully preserved the customs and usages of past times.

While Judaism in the whole of Europe is employing all its intelligence and all its activity in the completion of its great Talmud work, what is the fortune of the book among Christians? The Jews were persecuted; the work that was the soul of the unfortunate nation was not to be spared. "It has been proscribed, and imprisoned, and burnt, a hundred times over," says the author of the Quarterly Review article. "From Justinian, who, as early as 553 A.D., honored it by a special interdictory Novella (Novella 146), down to Clement VIII and later- a space of over a thousand years- both the secular and the spiritual powers, kings and emperors, popes and anti-popes, vied with each other in hurling anathemas and bulls and edicts of wholesale confiscation and conflagration against this luckless book." In 1239, Gregory IX has it burnt in France and in Italy; in 1264, Clement IV renews the prohibition, and condemns to the stake those who harbor manuscripts of it.

Two centuries later the interdict is not yet removed, and

## THE TALMUD

it took from 1484 to 1519, that is, thirty-six years, to print twenty-three treatises- the publication was secret. In 1520, Leo X abrogates the decree. But in 1553, at the instigation of the apostate Jew, Solomon Romano, Julius III again imposes the interdict, and has the Talmud burnt at Rome and at Venice. Paul IV, incited by Vittorio Eliano, the worthy brother of Romano, imitates Julius III in 1559. Four years later, the Council of Trent permits the publication of the Talmud, but under so close a surveillance by the censor that at first the Jews refuse to profit by the authorization. Not until 1578 does the Basle edition appear, "so expurgated that it might be read with profit even by Christians." But, though Pius VI in 1566 and Clement VIII in 1592 and 1599 renew the decrees of prohibition in spite of the Council, the editions of the Talmud multiply rapidly, and the sixteenth century, under the influence of the Reformation; sees Jewish studies in honor with Christian scholars, who seek the instruction of Rabbis. The most celebrated scholar of the sixteenth century is Reuchlin, the impartial savant, the intrepid champion of the Talmud.

Among others, there is Maximilian I's physician, Paul Riccio, the first, I believe, to attempt a Latin compilation of the Talmud. In the following century works abound. Above all should be cited those of the two Buxtorfs, who for more than seventy years occupy in succession the chair of Hebrew at Basle, and publish Hebrew grammars and lexicons, translate Jewish authors of the middle ages, and instruct their contemporaries in Rabbinic studies. Next, Latin translations of diverse Talmudic texts are attempted. Constant l'Empereur translates and annotates the treatises Baba Kamma and Middoth; Coccieus, the treatises Makkoth and Synhedrin; Surenhusius, the Mishna, which had been translated before into Spanish and Latin by the Jew Jacob and his brother Isaac Abendana. Selden publishes his learned studies on The Jewish Woman, the Civil Year, Natural Law according to the Hebrews, the Tribunals; Lightfoot issues his

# THE TALMUD

Hebraic and Talmudic Hours Shickard his Royal Law among the Hebrews,' snatched from Rabbinic Darkness;' Bartolocci, finally, his 'great Rabbinic library.' In the eighteenth century, we have among others the works of Wagenseil, Danz, Schoettgen, Rheinfeld, Egger.

But though these authors in various respects deserve commendation, the greater part of them write under the influence of religious prejudice or the narrowest fanaticism, and wittingly or unwittingly sacrifice truth to party spirit. Often religious passion is openly displayed, and has the frankness to announce itself in the very titles. Wagenseil, the learned translator of Sota, gives us his Fiery Datts of Satan, or, the Secret and Horrible Books of the Jews against Jesus Christ and the Christian Religion, and later, his Christian Denunciation of the Blasphemies of the Jews against Jesus Christ. Danz, the author of Rabbinism Explained, publishes, The Jews slain with their own Sword; Eisenmenger, Judaism Unmasked, or the Complete Account of the Calumnies, Blasphemies, Errors, and Fables of the Jews. Have such studies, inspired solely by ardent and malignant fanaticism, the rights of citizenship in the Republic of Letters?

The science of our day owes to itself the duty of studying the Talmud impartially. It will judge worthy of its attention this monument of a religion and a civilization whose influence has not been void in the world, and, whatever its absolute value may be adjudged to be, science will understand it, and study its formation and development. It will demand of the Talmud instruction, or at least information, almost as varied as the subjects coming within the compass of science. The historian will address himself to it for light upon the history of the early centuries of the Christian era and of the centuries immediately preceding it, and though not seeking in it precise data, which it cannot furnish, he will be sure to find a faithful picture of the

## THE TALMUD

beliefs and ideas of the Jewish nation, of its moral and spiritual life. The naturalist will ask of it numerous questions concerning the sciences, physical, natural, or medical. Has it ever occurred to any one to compile, if not the fauna, at least the flora of the Talmud, that is, of the Palestine and Babylonia contemporary with the Empire? It were easy with it as a basis to furnish a second edition of Pliny's Natural History, certainly as valuable as the first. The lawyer will question it on the history of its jurisprudence, will investigate whether, how, and by what intermediaries Roman law and Persian customs influenced it, and it will be a curious study to compare the results that two different civilizations, directed by opposite principles, have reached in the *Jus civile* and the *Jus Talmudicum*. The mythologist will dive into its legends, and, by a wise application of thecomparative method, determine the history of Midrashic mythology. The philologist will devote himself to the language- that abrupt, rough language, by means of which the Talmud seems to please itself in heaping up obscurities of form over those of the thought, and he will be sure to make more than one happy find. For, says the author of the History of the Semitic Languages, "the lexical spoliation and grammatical analysis of the Talmudic language, according to the methods of modern philology, remain to be made... That language fills a hiatus in the history of Semitic idioms." Finally, the philosopher will demand of the Talmud the explanation of Judaism and the history of Jewish institutions, and as the Talmudic books offer the completest expression thereof, and as he has at hand all the component elements, a scrupulous analysis will give him the law of the development of the Jewish religion.

## THE END

Printed in Great Britain
by Amazon